STORMING MONTE LA DIFENSA

The First Special Service Force at the Winter Line, Italy 1943

BRET WERNER

First published in Great Britain in 2015 by Osprey Publishing,
PO Box 883, Oxford, OX1 9PL, UK
PO Box 3985, New York, NY 10185-3985, USA
E-mail: info@ospreypublishing.com

Osprey Publishing is part of the Osprey Group

A CIP catalog record for this book is available from the British Library

Print ISBN: 978 1 4728 0766 3
PDF ebook ISBN: 978 1 47280 767 0
ePub ebook ISBN: 978 1 47280 768 7

Index by Alan Rutter
Typeset in Sabon
Maps by bounford.com
3D BEV by Alan Gilliland
Originated by PDQ Media, Bungay, UK
Printed in China through Worldprint Ltd

15 16 17 18 19   10 9 8 7 6 5 4 3 2 1

Osprey Publishing is supporting the Woodland Trust, the UK's leading
woodland conservation charity, by funding the dedication of trees.

www.ospreypublishing.com

ACKNOWLEDGEMENTS

I would like to thank John Dallimore of the First Special Service Force Living
History Group for supplying current photographs and information from his
trip to Mt Difensa. I would like to acknowledge Eric Morgensen for his
photographs and for administering the FSSF Association web site. I would
also like to thank Tricia Hofeld for providing photographs and answering
questions about her grandfather. I would also like to acknowledge
Judith Langston for donating photographs to me to be displayed by the
First Special Service Force Living History Group, as well as Jan Roll, who
always provides interesting information regarding the Force. I would
especially like to send my love and thanks to my wife Liz and my mother
Lyn for their continued support. Lastly, thanks and love to my daughter
Megan for always being an inspiration, never cease your passion of
learning.

DEDICATION

In memory of my father, Philip Werner.

IMPERIAL WAR MUSEUM COLLECTIONS

Many of the photos in this book come from the Imperial War Museum's
huge collections which cover all aspects of conflict involving Britain and
the Commonwealth since the start of the twentieth century. These rich
resources are available online to search, browse and buy at
www.iwmcollections.org.uk. In addition to Collections Online, you can visit
the Visitor Rooms where you can explore over 8 million photographs,
thousands of hours of moving images, the largest sound archive of its kind
in the world, thousands of diaries and letters written by people in wartime,
and a huge reference library. To make an appointment, call (020) 7416
5320, or e-mail mail@iwm.org.uk.

Imperial War Museum www.iwm.org.uk

CONTENTS

INTRODUCTION

It is common knowledge that the victory over Nazi Germany could only have been achieved by a strong alliance of nations that shared the same goals and war aims. No alliance in history was as strong or as equally committed to one another as the US–Anglo Alliance during World War II. In the course of the struggle, this alliance recognized the need for specially trained soldiers that could go above and beyond tasks the standard infantryman could be expected to do, and it would give birth to a fully integrated special operations force combining both Americans and Canadians – the First Special Service Force. In doing so, the alliance paved the way for future combined US, Canadian, British and Australian special operations forces that have continued a strong tradition of cooperation in conflicts around the world since the end of World War II.

Special operations forces were born out of the necessity for offensive actions in the early stages of the war. By the summer of 1940, Hitler's forces controlled the continent of Europe with the exception of Great Britain. The need for specially trained soldiers that could conduct raids behind enemy lines was considered vital to the war effort. Not only could these forces disrupt enemy operations by tying down thousand of troops and destroying vital strategic targets, they could also provide a much-needed boost in morale. Winston Churchill stated, "Enterprises must be prepared … with specially trained troops of the hunter class who can develop a reign of terror down these coasts" (Horn and Wyczynski, p.14–15). British Lt Col Dudley Clarke jumped at the idea of developing a special irregular force to conduct raids behind enemy lines. Based on the guerrilla concept gleaned from the Boer Kommandos during the Boer War, Clarke began to create his own commando units placed under the British Special Service Brigade. The Commandos would first fall under the Director of Combined Operations Admiral of the Fleet Sir Roger Keyes, who had gained fame for his raid on Zeebrugge during World War I (see Osprey Raid 7). Keyes would be replaced by Lord Louis Mountbatten in 1941 and given the title of Chief Advisor of

US Rangers advance under smoke in the mountains outside of Naples in October of 1943. Prior to the arrival of the Force, some of Fifth Army's most specialized troops were the Rangers. The Rangers were made up of the 1st, 3rd, and 4th Ranger battalions. Just prior to the Force's assault on Difensa, the 3rd Ranger Battalion made a feint towards San Pietro, where it encountered fierce opposition and was ordered to withdraw. The survivors of the 1st, 3rd and 4th Rangers after the assault on Cisterna would end up becoming members of the First Special Service Force in Anzio. (IWM NA 6999)

Combined Operations. Under Mountbatten, the commando program would be expanded to include special operations forces such as the Long Range Desert Group (LRDG) and the Special Air Service (SAS) to perform commando-type operations in North Africa and later in the Mediterranean theater of operations.

After entering the war, the United States would soon follow Britain's lead by creating its own specialized troops based on the commando model. In June of 1942 the first of the Ranger battalions was activated in Northern Ireland. A month later another very specialized force was created, which would be fully integrated with both Americans and Canadians. Lord Mountbatten needed a special operations force that could penetrate deep behind enemy lines by air, live for months in mountainous snow-covered regions, and destroy key enemy infrastructure. It could possibly be used to halt the German atomic weapons program by destroying the heavy water station at Rjukan in Norway. This commando unit, initially called the "Plough Force," would later be called the First Special Service Force (FSSF).

The Allied situation would start to change drastically throughout 1942, as the war would soon turn offensive in nature. By the spring of 1943 the fighting in North Africa had come to an end. The Soviets had been victorious at Stalingrad and were now slowly turning the momentum of the fighting against the German invaders. The tide had also turned against Germany in the Battle for the Atlantic, where the U-boats had become the hunted instead of the hunters. Across the world in the Pacific theater of operations, the Japanese were now on the defensive after the stunning US victories at Midway and Guadalcanal. By the fall of 1943, the Aleutians and New Guinea would be back in Allied hands.

With the defeat of Erwin Rommel and his famed Afrika Korps in the spring of 1943, attention was turned to an invasion of Europe: the question was where and when. President Roosevelt wanted a build-up of men and material in the United Kingdom for the cross-channel invasion known as Operation *Overlord*. Stalin wanted immediate action in Europe as his forces were still feeling the full brunt of the German onslaught in the Soviet Union. Churchill believed that an invasion of Italy would divert vital German resources and manpower away from the Russian front as well as distract attention from the forthcoming channel invasion. At Casablanca and later at the Trident conferences, the Allied leadership agreed that the invasion of Sicily must take place to knock Italy out of the war and divert as much of Germany's resources as possible away from the Normandy beaches and the Soviet Union.

The change from a defensive strategy of survival to an aggressive offensive posture would also see a change in the nature of special operations forces such as the commandos and the FSSF. The need for guerrilla tactics behind enemy lines to destroy infrastructure and to tie up resources was now overshadowed by the need for large well-equipped armies that could land vast amounts of troops in an effort to beat back the German war machine.

A Forceman makes a jump during the winter months at Ft Harrison. Here we can see the deployed white T-5 parachute. During the early days of training, the Forcemen were often referred to as "para-skiers" due to their paratroop training as well as their ski and winter warfare training. (National Archives)

This is not to say that special operations forces did not still have an important role to play, but instead they would now be used as a support element for the larger divisions and armies. These groups would still work behind the lines in many cases and be given special assignments, but now in the context of supporting a larger operation instead of being the operation themselves. The SAS and LRDG proved very effective at this in North Africa, but not every commander would use this vital resource effectively. Many old-guard generals who had cut their teeth in World War I never understood or fully recognized the potential of special operations forces. They were uncertain how to deploy or utilize these small groups of highly trained individuals. This would unfortunately be the fate of the First Special Service Force.

The First Special Service Force soon found itself in Italy, and not behind the lines in Norway destroying heavy water plants. Mt Difensa and Mt Camino were holding up the Fifth Army's advance into the Liri Valley, which was considered the gateway to Rome. For months Allied soldiers tried to take Mt Difensa, with no success. The Force would soon find itself being used as shock troops assaulting the impenetrable mountain position. Like other special operations forces, the need to use the FSSF behind enemy lines as guerrillas or commandos was not considered as urgent as the need for conventional targets to be eliminated. The Force would never be used for its intended purpose; instead it would build a legacy based on aggressive tactics and doing the job that would normally be assigned to much larger units. Fifth Army commanders are often criticized for not properly employing the FSSF and wasting the talents of this highly trained organization by using its members as shock troops. In many ways these criticisms are accurate, but hindsight is always twenty-twenty. Used properly or not, the FSSF always accomplished its missions, never retreating or giving up ground, and it exemplified the meaning of special forces.

ORIGINS

The birth of the First Special Service Force

The Mediterranean theater of operations was in not in anyone's mind when the First Special Service Force was first devised over a year earlier in 1942. Operation *Plough* was formulated by an eccentric British scientist named Geoffrey Pyke; the concept was to create an elite winter warfare commando force that could be dropped deep behind enemy lines and operate as a self-sufficient organization with little need for resupply. The initial target for this force was the Rjukan heavy water facility used for the German atomic weapons research program in Norway. Other potential targets included the Ploesti oil fields in Romania and the hydroelectric plants in the Italian Alps. Prime Minister Winston Churchill and the head of Combined Operations Lord Louis Mountbatten became keen proponents of such an operation. The need for a specialized snow vehicle was imperative if the operation was to be successful. Since no capable snow vehicle currently existed, and since Britain was not in a position to develop such a vehicle at that time, it was decided to offer Operation *Plough* to the United States. In March of 1942, the US Army Chief of Staff Gen Marshall accepted the *Plough* mission and immediately went to US auto manufactures with requests to start designing a snow vehicle that the "Plough Force" could use. This vehicle would later be called the T-15 light cargo carrier, or the "Weasel."

The Operation *Plough* feasibility study was then sent to Lt Col Robert T. Frederick of the Operations Division, US General Staff, where he determined the project to be flawed for several reasons, chiefly for its lack of an exit strategy for the raiders. Despite Frederick's warnings, the

ROBERT FREDERICK

Maj Gen Robert T. Frederick graduated from West Point in 1928, after which he was assigned to the Coastal Artillery. Frederick went on to attend Command and General Staff School, from where he graduated in 1939. In August of the same year Frederick was assigned to the War Plans Division of the War Department General Staff, where he was later given Project Plough to review. After Frederick gave the project a critical synopsis, the Pentagon decided to continue with the operation anyway. Frederick was then surprisingly given command of the Project Plough operation by General Eisenhower. The Plough Force would turn into the First Special Service Force in the summer of 1942. Frederick was promoted from colonel to brigadier general in January 1944 for his leadership at Mt Difensa. For his success at Anzio and in the campaign for Rome, Frederick was promoted to major general and given command of the First Airborne Task Force of which the FSSF was a part. In December of 1944, Frederick was given command of the 45th Infantry Division, making him the youngest divisional commander in the US Army at age 37. Frederick would retire from military service in 1951. Frederick always led from the front, as he expected all of his officers to do; he was wounded nine times during World War II, giving him notoriety as the general with the most Purple Heart medals. Frederick was loved by his men and feared by his enemies.

(US War Department)

War Department continued with its plans to create an elite commando force. The first officer chosen to lead the Plough Force quickly resigned due to personality conflicts with Geoffrey Pyke; it was then suggested by none other than Lord Mountbatten that Lt Col Frederick be given the commandos. Originally intended to be one-third American, one-third Canadian, and one-third Norwegian, it was soon realized that the Norwegian government in exile would be unable to provide sufficient manpower. The "Plough Force" would be solely an American and Canadian endeavor. In June of 1942, Canadian Prime Minister Mackenzie King approved the use of Canadian soldiers and in July of 1942, the Canadian Minister of National Defense James Ralston officially assigned 697 officers and enlisted men to the *Plough* project. Recruitment was rigid; Frederick needed a specific type of solider. Posters called for "single men between the ages of 21 and 35 who had completed three years or more grammar school within the occupational range of lumberjacks, forest rangers, hunters, northwoodsmen, game wardens, prospectors, and explorers" (Springer, p.3). These men would need to fight and survive in extreme winter conditions as well as be airborne qualified.

On July 20, 1942, the "Plough Force," now officially designated the First Special Service Force, was activated at Ft William Henry Harrison in Helena, MT. The United States government would furnish all uniforms, equipment, food, shelter, and travel expenses for the newly formed unit. The United States would also provide a service battalion to make available all necessary support elements, as the other regiments would focus solely on combat training. The Canadian soldiers would be fully integrated with the US forces, yet they would remain on paper as part of the Canadian military and were designated the 2nd Canadian Parachute Battalion, later changed to 1st Canadian Special Service Battalion.

Training

The training received by the First Special Service Force was arguably some of the most vigorous instruction in all the Allied armies. The initial training schedule fell into three parts: (1) August 3 to October 3 for parachute training, training in the basic subjects such as weapons, demolitions, small-unit tactics, and constant attention to reaching the peak of physical fitness; (2) October 5 to November 21 for unit tactics and problems; and (3) the remaining time which would be given over to skiing, rock climbing, living in cold climates and operation of the Force's new snow vehicle (the Weasel) (Burhans, p.23). 1st Lt Bill Story summarizes the training:

> We did calisthenics, extended calisthenics … We had the usual push ups and running from place to place, but we also did a lot of walking, a lot of simply walking over the hills and climbing up the mountains. It was excellent conditioning. There was mountaineering too. We went out with people who were trained mountaineers and who taught us how to climb using ropes, pitons, hammers, links, and the rest of it. We trained on rock faces, going up and rappelling down. We were intensely trained in demolitions … two or three nights a week we were in classrooms getting updates on map reading, land survival, plus the different techniques for using demolitions. (Springer, p.27)

One of the first tests the men would have to endure was jump training; it was also used as the first in many steps to weed out unfit candidates. It should be noted that the airborne training was modified from what was being taught at Ft Benning, Georgia. The FSSF only had to make two jumps to qualify; this was in the nature of saving time, since these men had so many other tasks to master. Lt Thomas recalled, "Two jumps for qualification instead of the five or six required in parachute school at Benning, and no night jumps. And no assembly on the ground, which of course, is the very essence of airborne operations … we weren't going to fight in big units, just small teams" (Springer, p.20).

Mountain climbing, hand-to-hand combat, land survival, map reading, small-unit tactics and scouting, and patrolling were just some of the daily exercises. Sgt Lewis remembered, "Those forced marches were long and deadly. They would be from twenty to thirty miles under full combat loads" (Springer, p.25–26). Hand-to-hand combat would be taught by Captain O'Neill. O'Neill, formerly the international police chief in Shanghai, was

brought to the US to work with the Office of Strategic Services (OSS) but instead wound up with an officer's commission and as the First Special Service Force's hand-to-hand expert. "O'Neill showed us how to kill easily using our hands, our feet, and utilizing the knife. All of it came in handy," according to Cpl Glass (Springer, p.36). Lt Story recalls:

> O'Neill's "Kick and poke" school of mayhem. Basically that is what he taught us. Unarmed combat was the effective use of a kick and the effective use of the hands into the lethal points, under the nose, throat, and neck. He also taught us how to use the garrote, a wire with toggles on the end. You could take a person's head off with that. I guess we were the first US unit that had this type of training. It was more extensive than the Brits taught in their commando schools. (Springer, p.35)

The ski training would be overseen by Norwegian Army skiers. Lt Story indicates, "The men got to be fairly capable skiers. The Norwegian training commander said that after a month or so the Force was as proficient as Norwegian conscripts were at the end of a year" (Springer, p.40). Weapons and demolitions were another expertise that the soldiers would master. They trained on almost every weapon in the US small-arms arsenal as well as becoming familiar with German weapons. The troops had no limits on ammunition and were free to go to the range during their off time to shoot as much as they liked. The men really enjoyed demolitions training; Sgt Lewis recounts, "Most of the guys got a little carried away with it, really.

Forcemen boarding a C-47 to make their airborne qualification jumps at Ft William Henry Harrison. Airborne qualification in the Force only required two jumps, unlike the five for standard parachute infantrymen. Jump training took about a week in the First Special Service Force; it was expected that these men would have to parachute into Norway for Operation *Plough*. It was not until Anzio that the Force started to take replacements without airborne qualifications. (National Archives)

Members of the First Special Service Force on a training march outside Helena, MT in the early fall of 1942. These marches were generally 20 to 30 miles long with full packs: notice that the men carry poles. These poles were used to simulate skiing, to get the men's shoulders in form for the real thing. These men wear the unusual training uniform of shorts, A-2 leather jackets, helmets and combat equipment. (Author's Collection/ FSSFLHG)

JULY 20, 1942

First Special Service Force is activated

They blew up bridges, culverts, and everything around Helena, Montana. Good God! I had never seen anything like it" (Springer, p.31). Pvt Minto verifies, "We were blowing so many structures to smithereens that we made a few mistakes here or there. We blew up a bridge … it was the wrong bridge. We blew up an old mine … we got the wrong mine. We blew the hell out of everything out there" (Springer, p.31).

The following excerpts from the War Diary, 2nd Canadian Parachute Battalion[1] (within First Special Service Force) detail some of the training.

8/24/42 Over 300 men were jumped this morning … 8/25/42 A bad day for jumpers, an unusually large number balked at the door. Casualties were also high compared to previous days.[2] 1 37 admitted to the hospital …

8/28/42 All companies in the force were instructed chiefly in all three American weapons

1 The 2nd Canadian Parachute Regiment was the designation in Canada for the First Special Service Force
2 It should be noted that all men were given a second chance to jump; if they refused they were removed from the Force. If you were injured during jumping you were also removed from the Force.

ORDER OF BATTLE

Headquarters Detachment
Service Battalion (300)
Combat Communications Detachment (4)
Headquarters Company (157)
Service Company (327)
w/Parachute Platoon
Maintenance Company (151)
Medical Detachment (19)
Cannon Company (spring 1944)

Regiments (609 each)
1st Regiment
2nd Regiment
3rd Regiment

Regimental Breakdown
Regimental Headquarters (6)
Regimental Supply Detachment (19)
Regimental Medical Detachment (2)
Col Commanding, Lt Col 2nd in Command

2 Battalions per regiment (291 per battalion)
Battalion Headquarters (6)
Lt Col Commanding, Major 2nd in Command

3 Companies per battalion (95 per company)
Company Headquarters (5)
Captain Commanding, 1st Lt 2nd in Command

3 Platoons per company (30 per platoon)
Platoon Headquarters (2)
Mortar Team (4)
1st Lt Commanding, Platoon Sgt 2nd in Command

2 Sections per platoon (12 per section)
S/Sgt Section Leader

*Section Breakdown***

S/Sgt Section Leader
Sgt Demolitions
Sgt Demolitions
Sgt Demolitions
Tech 4 Radioman
Tech 4 First Aid
Tech 4 Navigator
Tech 4 Mechanic
Tech 4 Mechanic
Pvt
Pvt
Pvt

*Please note that the numbers are averages; the Force was usually under strength, but at times did become over strength.
**The section did not always keep this composition, especially after large amounts of replacements filled the ranks.

mainly (1) Machine Gun (2) The Garand M1 rifle (3) The Browning Automatic Rifle …
10/6/42 The officers, picked for advance study demolitions, left at 0700 hours to blow up a bridge near Butte … The first regiment left at 0700 hours on a force march 36 miles – to Marysville and return – full equipment …
11/2/42 Training this week will cover bayonet drill, firing of L.M.G., Thompson S.M.G., pistol, rifle and motor school. Ski training (8 hours by the end of the week for everyone) the daily run of the obstacle course …
11/23/42 Training continues with a view of developing all units from the section to the regiment into a highly mobile organization prepared to accomplish successfully the following types of combat MISSIONS: a) Operate against vital military and industrial targets. b) Operate as an overland training force infiltrating, penetrating or encircling deep into enemy territory to destroy important targets. c) Operate as a spearhead in forcing strongly fortified localities with the expectation of early support from friendly troops. d) Operate in cold or mountainous regions to accomplish any or all of the possible missions.
2/1/43 … Training for the week will cover: 1st Rgt., Field Fortifications in the snow, Rifle, L.M.G., Mortar, and Antiaircraft firing, platoon combat proficiency tests, instruction on

anti tank rocket; 2nd Regt. Will have field exercises from Tues to Sat inclusive; 3rd Regt., Field Fortifications in snow, a field exercise. (Cited by Wood, p.194–98)

It was the training that made the Force such a potent entity on the battlefield; it was the training that made them specialists in the art of warfare, and it was the training that would keep many alive in very perilous situations. According to Sgt Wright, "The training was tough, but it sure got us in shape … we crawled through entanglements with machinegun fire going above our heads. … it was at night … and a good initiation to enemy fire, which we certainly experienced later on" (Springer, p.28). 2nd Lt Radcliff concurs that "Another thing that saved our necks was the constant night training. We were trained never to make an approach or an attack in the daylight. We did night training all of the time … We would be up on a mountain … and another regiment would attack us in the dark and we would defend the mountain" (Springer, p.26).

In October of 1942, Operation *Plough* was canceled and the future of the First Special Service Force was now in question. Training continued and was expanded to meet the needs of several types of potential missions. Frederick, in a memorandum to the Deputy Chief of Staff dated February 3, 1943, wrote:

The time has been reached when it is necessary to decide the future of the First Special Service Force. The First Special Service Force was created specifically for the accomplishment of the Plough Project at the request of the British authorities, but in October, 1942, the project was dropped due to the impracticability of executing it during the winter of 1942–43. Reasons for abandoning the project were the planning information furnished by the British mission assigned to the project was faulty and erroneous, airplanes to drop the Force into the combat area are not available, and the Norwegian Government did not favour the project or its objective … Considering the capabilities of this Force and the limitations upon its use, one of the following missions offers the most profitable use and should be decided upon at this time: a. participation in an operation in the Aleutian Islands, if one is to be undertaken during the spring of 1943 … b. Transfer of the Force to the United Kingdom for employment to the Continent of Europe as a raiding force …. c. Assignment of the Force to North Africa and employment as a raiding force either in Africa or in the Mediterranean area. (Cited by Wood, p.60–61)

General Marshall wanted to keep the Force alive as a special operations formation if a mission could be found. With the rumors spreading of possibly disbanding this elite force, Winston Churchill finally weighed in:

On no account dissipate PLOUGH force. Nothing could be more improvident than to yield to the natural impatience of the highly competent teams employed. Their chance will come and may alter the whole strategic position of the war, whereas to break them up now is to blot out large strategic possibilities in the future. (Cited by Joyce 2006, p.113)

General Eisenhower was considering using the First Special Service Force in the Mediterranean theater of operations and wrote "that the unit should be amphibiously trained and should maintain its parachute proficiency until such a time as he [Eisenhower] could determine its exact method of employment" (Wood p.62). On April 11, 1943, the First Special Service Force was transferred to Norfolk, Virginia for amphibious training. It was here that they broke the US Marines' record for loading into landing craft from transport ships, as remembered by Lt. Col. Burhans regarding an unidentified naval ensign that was present: "'These night loadings are the real test. The best Army division averaged about one minute per platoon load from the first man over to the time the boat pulled away. Of course, the Marines did it in about 52 seconds. That's the best we've seen.' ... A Third Regiment boat load, the first one over the side, was down the ropes and the boat pulled away with an elapsed time ... of exactly 33 seconds" (Burhans, p.55–56). Colonel Howe, the XO of the training center, commented on the Force's ability as follows: "The Special Service Force, because of its organization, the superior type of personnel, their varied training, and their extreme mobility, are ideally suited for assignment as assault waves of a ship to shore operation ... [With additional jungle warfare training] these troops would become the most versatile and most effective combat troops in any army." The men of the First Special Service Force were now qualified paratroops, ski and mountain troops, and amphibious troops, as well as demolition and weapons experts.

On April 6, 1943, the First Special Service Force made a farewell march down Last Chance Gulch in Helena, MT just prior to being sent to Norfolk, Virginia for amphibious training. Here we see Lt Goodwin 6-1 (just left of center) in his Canadian officer uniform with American equipment. Notice that the officers carry folding-stock airborne carbines. The officer in the center wears a US officer's uniform while the officer to the right wears a Canadian uniform, testifying to the complete integration of the members of the Force. 6th Company, 2nd Battalion, 1st Regiment photographed here was battered by mortar and artillery fire while being held in reserve below Mt Difensa. Lt Goodwin's carbine was shattered by a round and the company suffered heavy casualties. (Photographed by BJ Dahl, Courtesy of Eric Morgensen/www.firstspecialserviceforce.net)

After amphibious training in Virginia, the Force went on to Ft Ethan Allen, Vermont in May of 1943 to hone their combat skills and wait for an assignment. The men were starting to grow impatient after almost a full year of training and no mission. The May 28, 1943 entry in the 2nd Canadian Parachute Battalion War Diary explains:

> Col Frederick explained the reason for the many changes in training had been the changing of the mission for the Force. He said that one day in Washington within 14 hours the Force had been assigned to 6 different missions. At present the Force was not assigned to any mission but it was sufficiently trained that it must expect to be alerted at any time and leave with little notice. (Cited by Wood, p.200)

This prediction would come true when the FSSF was unexpectedly ordered to San Francisco at the beginning of June 1943 to be assigned to Amphibious Training Force No. 9 for the invasion of Kiska, in the Aleutian Islands, off the coast of Alaska, which were occupied by the Japanese.

Organization

The First Special Service Force combat echelon was broken down into three regiments, each under a colonel. Each regiment had two battalions, commanded by a lieutenant colonel. Within each battalion were three companies, led by a captain. A company was made up of three platoons.

TRAINING SYLLABUS

The following training syllabus was labeled "First Canadian Special Service Battalion"

Specialized Training

Qualified Parachutist
Army Skiing, 6 weeks
Mountain warfare, 3 weeks
Amphibious landings and Rubber boats, 6 weeks
Demolitions, 2 months
Special Recce Track Vehicles, 1 month

Tactics and United States Weapons

M-1 Rifle .30
Pistol .45
Rifle Grenade
Flame Thrower
Johnson Automatic Rifle
Browning Automatic Rifle
Thomson Submachine Gun
Browning LMG
Anti-Tank Rocket Launcher
Mortar 60mm
All purpose Grenades US
Chemical Warfare
Radio Operator
First Aid

JUNE 1943

FSSF begins preparation for invasion of Aleutian Islands

A platoon was led by a lieutenant, and was made up of two sections. A section was originally designed with nine men in mind in order to crew the Weasel, but after the *Plough* operation was canceled it would later be expanded to 12 men led by a staff sergeant. The section was the fundamental fighting formation of the First Special Service Force. Each regiment was assigned a small supply detachment, medical detachment, and combat communications detachment.

The service battalion was made up of three companies. Headquarters Company was administrative; it included the intelligence section, radio operators, and the military police platoon. The Maintenance Company was in charge of all equipment maintenance. The Service Company was composed of the parachute riggers, the Field Music Detachment, supply troops, the cooks, and any other support specialists. The FSSF Service Battalion was wholly made up of Americans, and though they were intended to serve as rear support troops, these men would sometimes find themselves in the thick of battle, bringing supplies to the front, acting as stretcher bearers, and fighting as riflemen.

INITIAL STRATEGY

The Allies' road to Rome

Operation *Husky*, the invasion of Sicily on July 10, 1943, was a combined US and British operation under the command of General Eisenhower. Palermo fell on July 24, and the next day the Italian dictator, Mussolini, was relieved by King Victor Emmanuel III. The king's replacement, Marshal Badoglio, began secret negotiations with the Allies. By August 16, General Patton was marching into Messina and the Germans had tactically withdrawn to the Italian mainland. In early September, Marshal Badoglio had signed an armistice with the Allies, thus prompting the Germans to move soldiers into Rome and other key strategic positions on the mainland of Italy.

JULY 10, 1943

Invasion of Sicily begins

Field Marshal Albert Kesselring was the German overall commander in the Mediterranean theater of operations. Kesselring was the mastermind behind the series of strong defensive lines that ran across Italy, including the Bernhardt and Gustav lines that made up the Winter Line in which Mt Difensa would play a prominent role. Kesselring ensured the Allies paid for every yard of soil taken during the Italian campaign, making him a legendary figure when it comes to the doctrine of defensive tactics. (Bundesarchiv, Bild 183-2005-0103-505, photo: o.Ang)

Field Marshal Kesselring had been given command of the German defense in southern Italy, while Field Marshal Erwin Rommel was given command of the northern Italian defenses. Rommel would eventually be reassigned to France where he would be in charge of the protection of Normandy against a potential Allied invasion, thus giving Kesselring complete control of Italy. In the south Kesselring had at his disposal three divisions: the 16th Panzer Division, which was to defend Salerno and the south, the Hermann Göring Division, which held the Naples plain, and the 15th Panzer Grenadier Division, which was north of Naples. Together they formed the German Tenth Army under the direct command of General Heinrich von Vietinghoff.

Operation *Avalanche* and the initial attack on the Winter Line

On September 3, 1943, the British Eighth Army crossed the straits of Messina as part of Operation *Baytown*, encountering little resistance, while the British 1st Airborne Division made an amphibious landing at Taranto in Operation *Slapstick*. The British 5th Division moved up the western coast while the Canadian 1st Division crossed the toe of the Italian boot and moved up the eastern coast to link up with the British 1st Airborne Division. The US Fifth Army under Lt Gen Mark Clark landed at Salerno on September 9 and encountered stiff resistance as part of Operation *Avalanche*. The invasion force consisted of the British 46th and 56th divisions, the British 2nd and 41st Commando, the US 36th Division, three US Ranger battalions under Lt Col Darby, and two regimental combat teams of the 45th Division held in reserve. The 82nd Airborne would jump into Salerno on September 14 to reinforce the beachhead. Field Marshal Kesselring's forces made several counterattacks on the

Members of the 15th Panzer Grenadier Division in full packs push through undergrowth in Sicily. It would be many of these same men that the Force faced on Mt Difensa. Veteran members of the 15th Panzer Grenadiers were part of the 15th Panzer, an original formation of the Afrika Korps, which was later reformed as the Division Sizilien and later again as the 15th Panzer Grenadiers. (IWM MH 6301)

beachhead for a week; unable to dislodge the Allies, he ordered a delaying action and an orderly withdrawal starting on September 16. By September 19 elements of the British Eighth Army began to link up with the US Fifth Army at Auletta, and the beachhead was consolidated and the resupply effort began.

Kesselring began to create his famous defensive lines that would run across Italy; they proved to be a formidable obstacle and a true deterrent to the Allied liberation of Rome. The first of these defenses was the Barbara Line, a set of loosely tied-together positions along the Volturno River. The second much more formidable line was the Bernhard Line (sometimes referred to as the Reinhard Line). This defensive line ran from Mt Camino and Mt Maggiore to Mt Sammucro, tying into Mt Cassino and the Gustav Line. The Gustav Line, anchored by Mt Cassino and running along the Garigliano and Rapido rivers, was the heaviest fortified of the defensive lines, with bunkers and strong defensive positions. Together these lines would be called the "The Winter Line" by the Allied forces. Kesselring ordered Vietinghoff to hold the Allied advances south of the Barbara Line as long as possible so that the Gustav Line could be primed.

Naples and the Volturno River were the Fifth Army's next objectives. Encountering stiff German rearguard delaying actions, the Allies paid for every mile of terrain acquired. On October 1, the 82nd Airborne and Darby's Rangers entered the ruined city of Naples; by October 7, the British X Corps had taken up positions along the Volturno River. Montgomery's Eighth Army in the east had taken the Foggia airfield and the port city of Termoli, thus bringing Operation *Avalanche* to a close. The Allies suffered heavy casualties in the operation, roughly 12,500 killed, wounded, and missing.

The assault across the Volturno River toward the Barbara Line occurred on October 13; the Germans fought fierce delaying actions as part of their planned withdrawal to the Bernhard Line. It took the US Fifth and British Eighth armies 20 days to move roughly 20 miles along a 40-mile front. The Germans, practicing a scorched-earth policy, destroyed everything they could upon withdrawing. The rain and mud also made movement and resupply extremely difficult. The Allies were eventually able to breach the Barbara Line, pushing as far as the base of the Bernhard Line. It was here that Gen Clark decided to make a push into the Liri Valley.

The Fifth Army would have to push through the Mignano Gap towards Mt Cassino in order to gain access to the Liri Valley. The Mignano Gap was heavily defended by Mts Camino, Difensa, and Lungo on the left side of the valley and Mts Sammucro and Rotondo on the right. The British 56th Division would assault Mt Camino while the US 3rd Division would breach the Mignano Gap, attacking Mt Lungo and Mt Rotondo while sending the 7th Infantry Regiment against the southern slopes of Mt Difensa. On November 5, the British 56th and the US 3rd divisions made their attacks against the Camino–Difensa front, both encountering stiff enemy resistance. While the British were able to take Calabritto at the base of Mt Camino, they were unable to make any gains on the summit.

US troops enter a rubble-filled street in Naples. On October 1, 1943, the 82nd Airborne Division along with the Darby's Ranger Battalions first entered the city after a local rebellion led by Italian partisans helped to keep the city from being totally destroyed by the retreating Germans. Lt Gen Clark made the Volturno River north of the city the objective for the Fifth Army. (IWM TA 2142)

The 3rd Division was having an equally hard time with the Difensa, Lunga, and Rotondo defenses. After days of fighting, Mt Lungo and Mt Rotondo were in Allied hands and the Germans had fallen back to San Pietro. The men fighting on Mt Difensa were not so lucky; for ten days the 7th Infantry Regiment attempted to take the summit in the freezing rain and snow. The 7th Infantry fought an almost futile uphill battle against the entrenched German Panzer grenadiers, who used the terrain masterfully. Taking the observable approach from the south, German snipers, mortars, grenades, and machine guns were able to pound the infantrymen as they tried to make their way up the slopes, so that the task was nearly impossible.

Orders were issued to withdraw along the entire Camino–Difensa front to the initial starting points of November 12. By the 15th, the 7th Regiment was back at the base of Difensa. The Allies were on the verge of exhaustion and no replacements could be spared due to the build-up for Operation *Overlord*. On November 15, the Fifth Army halted its advance so that the troops could consolidate their newly acquired positions, recuperate, resupply, and reorganize. The German defensive lines had proved to be more formidable than had been expected. The key to the Mignano Gap was Mt Difensa, and Gen Clark needed to find a unit that could crack its defenses and open a pathway to Rome. Little did he know that this force was on its way.

Debut of the Force

Three months earlier, the First Special Service Force had spearheaded an amphibious landing on Kiska in the Aleutian Islands against the Japanese, who had in fact deserted the island three days before the Force's arrival. The 1st and 3rd regiments used small rubber boats to assault the island. The 1st Regiment spearheaded the invasion on August 15 with the 3rd Regiment landing the next day. The 2nd Regiment waited as a ready reserve to parachute in or land by boats if needed. While no combat experience was gained, it did provide an excellent training operation. Maj Gen Corlett of the Western Defense Command praised the Force for its professionalism throughout the operation:

SEPTEMBER 3, 1943

Allies invade mainland Italy

> In the occupation of the Island of Kiska, the FSSF was under my command. They performed all missions according to plan and even though no actual enemy was encountered, their missions were difficult and dangerous. They landed with rubber boats at unknown beaches during hours of darkness against what was presumed to be hostile shore. They moved across difficult terrain and positions where cleverly concealed traps had been left by the enemy. They reached their objectives on schedule according to plan. To accomplish their mission it was impractical for them to carry packs to provide the ordinary comforts of soldiers in the field. As a consequence they were exposed to extreme discomfort for long periods of time. It is desired to commend all officers and men of the FSSF for their fine spirit and unselfishness. It is especially desired to commend Colonel Robert T. Frederick for his splendid leadership and devotion to duty. Colonel Frederick has a force that should be of great value in almost any difficult battle situation. (Cited by Horn and Wyczynski, p.161–62)

Little did Maj Gen Corlett know how true his sentiments would become in the near future. With no Japanese to fight, the Force was immediately ordered back to the United States on the first available transport by the highest authorities. Eager for an assignment that would utilize their skills and training, Col Robert T. Frederick began to mobilize his force of American and Canadian special forces. In September the Force was back at Ft Ethan Allen in Vermont preparing for its next mission. While nothing official had been stated, the men were given lectures on the Italian people and customs, training was intensified, last-minute promotions were made, and replacements were brought in. Something big was coming, but no one knew just what. On October 28, 1943, the First Special Service Force departed from Hampton Roads, Virginia, as it had been ordered by Gen Eisenhower to the Mediterranean theater of operations.

NOVEMBER 15, 1943

Fifth Army halts to consolidate positions

THE PLAN

Highest authority directs that you return Special Service Force to San Francisco without delay. NIMITZ
(Cited by Burhans, p.82)

A role for the FSSF

While the Force was in the Aleutians preparing for the invasion of Kiska, Mountbatten and the Combined Operations Staff were coming up with creative ways to use the former Plough Force in Europe. The Quadrant Conference, a top-secret meeting between the United States, Canada, and Great Britain, happened in Quebec on August 12, 1943. It was here that it was decided to proceed with Operation *Overlord*, better-known as D-Day. Churchill also made the case for a strong Allied effort in Italy. In a memo dated August 8, 1943 to the Combined Operations committee, Mountbatten stated:

> Have examined employment of PLOUGH force in Central Europe in conjunction with either a diversionary Operation in the South of France to help OVERLORD or an advance from Northern Italy on Vienna. Snow conditions in Alps are suitable from New Year to late April or May but terrain generally too steep for the vehicle and Force must be employed mainly as Para-Ski Troops. Probable Ski Troop opposition in this Area renders Force too small for independent role. It could therefore be used only in local operations in support of our main effort. (Cited by Joyce, p.145)

Several ideas were conceived as to the proper use of the Force. It was proposed as a diversionary unit that could screen the main attacking force, or its troops could parachute in prior to the main attack and hold or destroy vital targets, or they could work with or as a guerrilla force behind enemy lines. It was decided at the Quadrant Conference to see how things would play out in Italy and to bring the Force back to the States from the Aleutians as soon as possible.

On August 24, 1943 the War Department sent the following memo to Gen Eisenhower, the commander in the Mediterranean theater of operations, and to Lt Gen Francis Morgan, Chief of Staff for the Supreme Allied Command, regarding the FSSF.

Consists of combat echelon of units with strengths as follows: HQ of 12; 3 regiments of 417 each; air detachment of 8; and communications detachment of 4. Also a base echelon service battalion as follows; HQ and HQ Co 132; service Co 273; maint Co 126; and med det of 15. Unit has extended mountain, winter and commando type training, and limited amphibious and parachute training. Unit has highest morale and participated amphibiously as a unit in Kiska landings. It is well qualified for guerrilla activities in rugged snow terrain. Unit is equipped with normal infantry equipment, parachutes for men and equipment, and winter warfare equipment. Unit is authorized 600 T 24 carriers [the Weasels], which will be available by 1 December. These vehicles are tracked amphibious vehicles capable of operations at moderate speeds over hilly and snow covered terrain and capable of being parachuted from a C-54 or Lancaster. Unit has armament rifles, carbines, rocket launchers, light mgs and 60mm mortars. (Cited by Joyce, p.146)

Eisenhower was eager to get the First Special Service Force for use in Italy, and on September 16, the US Chiefs of Staff sent a request to London asking that the Force be placed under his command immediately. On October 28 the First Special Service Force embarked from Hampton Roads for Naples, Italy via North Africa. By November 19 the Force was making its way to its new home in Santa Maria. The 2nd Canadian Parachute Battalion War Diary indicates "Our destination was an Italian Military Academy built in 1935 … The Germans [the Hermann Göring Division] had used it for the past 3 years and did a very thorough job of willful destruction before leaving: all windows broken, plumbing destroyed and wall smashed, but even so one could see it had been a very fine school" (cited by Wood, p.202). On November 22, the Force was assigned to Fifth Army, II Corps under Maj Gen Geoffrey Keyes, who then assigned the Force to Maj Gen Fred Walker of the 36th Division. The 36th Division had arrived to replace the weary 3rd Division on November 16.

Immediately upon arriving at their new home at the Santa Maria barracks, Col Frederick ordered each regiment to send out patrols and become acquainted with their new surroundings. The 2nd Canadian Parachute Battalion War Diary reflects "A patrol made up of representatives of regiments and Force H.Q. left in the afternoon to operate over hills assigned as our mission to clear of German opposition. These hills are strongly and stubbornly defended, and are holding up the progress of the 5th Army" (cited by Wood, p.202). The men of the Force were also given orientation on mines and booby troops that were common in the area by men of the 36th Division.

The Winter Line quagmire

General Clark's ordered standstill during the last two weeks of November 1943 allowed the men of the Fifth Army to get some rest and consolidate

22 NOVEMBER 1943

FSSF is assigned to Fifth Army

Opposite: The plans for Operation Raincoat.

their positions. It also allowed Clark and his staff to work out a plan for an all-out assault on the Winter Line. In terms of the tactical situation, the Fifth Army had to precede into the Liri Valley, in order to take Rome. The obstacles in front of the Fifth Army were indeed formidable. To the south, from the coast up to the Liri Valley following the Garigliano River, were incredibly steep mountain ranges. At the mouth of the Garigliano River was a flood plain that was, unknowingly to the Allies, already causing the enemy problems with supplies and movement. The center of the Fifth Army faced the Mignano Gap, a natural throughway to the Liri Valley that extended towards Mt Cassino and then on to Rome. Highway 6 ran right through the gap, which narrowed to just about a mile at the town of Mignano. On either side of the gap lay a series of alarming mountain ranges that ran from north to south. The Camino mountain mass lay to the south of the gap encompassing Mt Camino, Mt Difensa, Mt Remetanea, and Mt Maggiore. In the center of the gap lay the smaller mountains of Mt Rotondo, which the Allies had been able to capture, and Mt Lungo. North of the Mignano Gap, protecting the Liri Valley on the right flank, the Fifth Army faced Mt Sammucro, Mt Radicosa, Mt Vischiataro, and Mt Majo. The Germans dominated this high ground, knowing that the only way into the valley was to seize these impenetrable heights. Every trail through the mountains was zeroed in by mortars and machine guns from higher ground. In the lower-lying areas, such as in the gap itself, strong points were created, mine fields were laid and bridges were destroyed.

The Fifth Army front was spread along the Garigliano Valley to Mt Sammucro. The British X Corps held the southern flank, which extended from the sea along the Garigliano Valley up to the base of the Camino mass. The US II Corps held the area from the base of the Camino mass across the Mignano Gap to Mt Rotonda. VI Corps held the northern flank, which started in Cannavinelle and led to the base of Mt Sammucro. Facing the

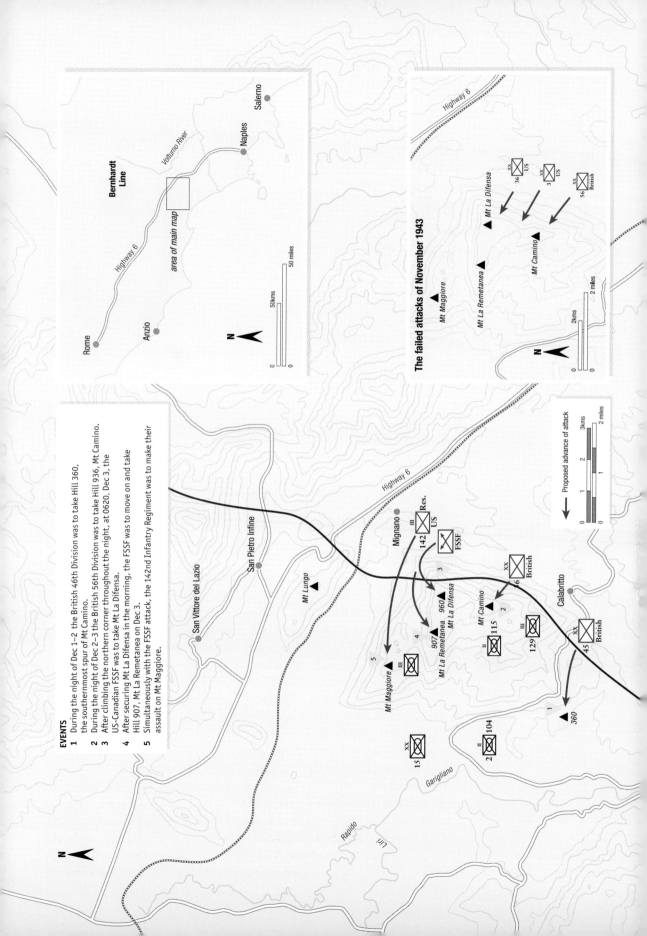

EVENTS

1 During the night of Dec 1–2 the British 46th Division was to take Hill 360, the southernmost spur of Mt Camino.
2 During the night of Dec 2–3 the British 56th Division was to take Hill 936, Mt Camino.
3 After climbing the northern corner throughout the night, at 0620, Dec 3, the US-Canadian FSSF was to take Mt La Difensa.
4 After securing Mt La Difensa in the morning, the FSSF was to move on and take Hill 907, Mt La Remetanea on Dec 3.
5 Simultaneously with the FSSF attack, the 142nd Infantry Regiment was to make their assault on Mt Maggiore.

Bernhardt Line

Rome
Anzio
Naples
Salerno
Volturno River
Highway 6
area of main map

50 miles
50kms

The failed attacks of November 1943

Highway 6
Mt La Difensa
Mt La Remetanea
Mt Camino
Mt Maggiore
36 US
3 US
56 British

2kms
2 miles

San Vittore del Lazio
San Pietro Infine
Mt Lungo
Mignano
Highway 6
Res. US
142
FSSF
3
Mt La Remetanea 907
Mt La Difensa 960
Mt Maggiore
5
4
Mt Camino 2
115
6 British
129
III
Calabritto
45 British
360 1
104 2
15
Garigliano
Rapido
Liri

→ Proposed advance of attack

3kms
2 miles

The Mignano Gap is clearly visible in this photograph as a natural opening in the mountainous German Winter Line defenses. With highway No. 6 running down the center towards Rome, control of the gap was essential for the Allies if they were to be able to move their tanks and supplies on to Rome. The Germans, being fully aware of this prospect, defended the Mignano Gap by placing crack troops on top of Mt Camino, Mt Difensa (960), Mt Mignano, Mt Lungo, Mt Sammucro, and of course Mt Cassino. By dominating the high ground, the Germans made the Allies pay for every yard in blood. (National Archives)

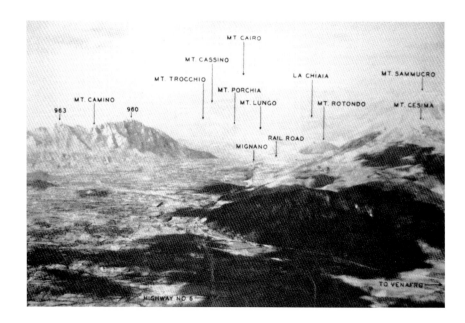

Fifth Army was the veteran German XIV Panzer Corps, at the time under the command of General von Senger und Etterlin. The XIV Corps consisted of the 94th Division that faced the British X Corps, the 15th Panzer Grenadier Division that held the center against the US II Corps up to around Mignano, and the 29th Panzer Grenadier Division that held from roughly Mignano to Venafro, with the 44th Grenadiers in the VI Corps front. The Hermann Göring Division was being held ready in reserve to reinforce where needed.

Gen Clark divided the proposed attack into three phases. The first phase would target the left of the Mignano Gap, focusing on Mt Camino, Mt Difensa, Mt Remetanea, and Mt Maggiore. The second phase would target the right of the Mignano Gap, focusing on Mt Lungo, Mt Sammucro, Mt Vischiataro, and Mt Majo. The final phase of the operation would be an all-out push into the Liri Valley. During the first phase of the operation, the British X Corps was to feint along the Garigliano River and capture Mt Camino, the US II Corps was to assault Mt Difensa, Mt Remetanea, Mt Maggiore, and to secure the mouth of the Mignano Gap, while VI Corps was to feint with aggressive patrols towards its front.

Planning and preparation for the first phase (Operation *Raincoat*)

The Camino mass of Mt Camino (Hill 963), Mt Difensa (Hill 960), Mt Remetanea (Hill 907) and Mt Maggiore (Hill 630) were the primary targets of the first phase, codenamed Operation *Raincoat*. The Camino mass had to be taken if the Allies were to gain control of the Mignano Gap; without it the other phases of the operation were useless and any drive forward on to Cassino and then Rome would be impossible. The Mt Camino summit was topped by a heavily defended monastery. Less than two miles to the north of Camino were the heavily defended Mt Difensa and Mt Remetanea, and just north of

Remetanea lay the lower peaks of Mt Maggiore. Together the Camino mass area was roughly six miles long and four miles wide (US War Dept, p.17).

While feints would be made both north and south of the Camino mass, the main assault would be made directly on Camino, Difensa, and Maggiore by the British 10 Corps and the US II Corps. The operation was to kick off on the night of December 1–2, with an attack against Hill 360 (the southernmost point of Mt Camino) by the British 46th Division. The British 56th Division would then assault the heights of Mt Camino on the night of December 2–3. At 0620 on December 3, the First Special Service Force was slated to assault Mt Difensa from the northeast corner departing from Hill 368, then move on to capture Mt Remetanea. The 142nd Regimental would assault Mt Maggiore at the same time, also departing from Hill 368. The success of this action depended entirely on each unit accomplishing its mission. If the 56th Division failed on Camino, then Difensa would be open to enemy fire from the high ground. If the FSSF failed on Difensa, then Remetanea and Difensa would remain in enemy hands, giving the Germans the high ground over Mt Maggiore and thus making any success on Camino useless as well. If the 142nd failed on Maggiore, the Germans would still dominate the Mignano Gap, making Phase 2 even more difficult.

Fifth Army engineers cleared mines and built bridges, roads and footpaths leading to the base of the mountains. Also, at the base of the Camino mass supply dumps were created with food, water, and ammunition as well as newly fashioned aid stations. Artillery was brought up en masse for what would become the largest concentrated barrage yet in the Italian theater of operations. Given the poor weather conditions, the XII Air Support Command would launch as many sorties as possible leading up to the assault, hitting targets such as bridges and other enemy infrastructure in the Liri Valley and on the Camino mass itself.

The feints intended to mislead the Germans as to where the actual assault would take place were launched in the last days of November. The British X Corps feinted along the Garigliano River valley, while VI Corps made aggressive diversionary attacks towards Mt Sammucro. The 3rd Ranger Battalion made a reconnaissance patrol in force towards San Pietro on the night of November 29; the Rangers encountered fierce resistance at dawn on the outskirts of the town and were ordered to withdraw that night once the sun had set.

At First Special Service Force Headquarters in Santa Maria, Col Frederick was working out plans for how he would accomplish his objective of taking Mt Difensa (Hill 960). It was decided that the 2nd Regiment would lead the assault, as they were the troops left on the runway with parachutes during the Kiska invasion. Once the summit was seized, the

The original plans for Operation *Raincoat*, the storming of Mt Camino, Mt Difensa, Mt Remetanea, and Mt Maggiore. The British 46th Division was to hit Hill 360, the southernmost tip of the Camino mass. The British 56th Division would attack Camino straight on, and the First Special Service Force had to tackle Mt Difensa and then move swiftly on to Mt Remetanea. The 142nd Infantry Regiment of the US 36th Division would attack Mt Maggiore. Operation Raincoat's success depended upon all elements accomplishing their missions: if one objective was left under enemy control, the entire operation was comprised. (National Archives)

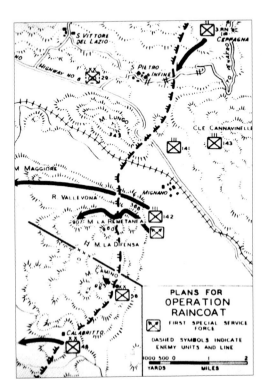

PLANS FOR
OPERATION
RAINCOAT

FIRST SPECIAL SERVICE FORCE

DASHED SYMBOLS INDICATE ENEMY UNITS AND LINE

1000 500 0

YARDS   MILES

FIFTH ARMY ORDER OF BATTLE DECEMBER 1943

Fifth Army Lt Gen Mark Clark
1st, 3rd, 4th Ranger Battalions
1st Italian Motorized Group
504th Parachute Infantry Regiment
II Corps Maj Gen Geoffrey Keyes
36th Division
3rd Division
1st Armored Division
First Special Service Force
VI Corps Maj Gen John Lucas
45th Division with 157th, 179th, 180th Regimental
Combat Teams

2nd Moroccan Division (transferred to French Corps on
Jan 3, 1944)
34th Division with 133rd, 135th, 168th Regimental
Combat Teams (transferred to II Corps on Dec 24)
10 Corps (British) Lt Gen Sir Richard McCreery
46th Division
56th Division
23rd Armored Brigade
French Expeditionary Corps Gen Alphonse Juin
3rd Algerian Division

1st Regiment would push through the 2nd Regiment and move on to take Mt Remetanea (Hill 907). The 3rd Regiment would be kept in reserve and used as supply and stretcher bearers. Frederick also sent out several patrols to locate the best positions to launch the attack. Maj Thomas, the executive officer of the 1st Battalion, 2nd Regiment, recalled:

> In the later part of November 1943, he [Lt Col MacWilliam] assigned me the task of leading the reconnaissance to select our attack route to the top of Difensa. 1st Company was chosen to lead the attack. My recon party included … the lead scouts from [1st Company] … Howard Van Ausdale and Tom Fenton. Van Ausdale had Indian blood in his background and was endowed with a superb sense of terrain, so I leaned on him heavily for advice. We both worked out a route up the mountain, but he was probably most responsible for the selection. (Springer, p.69)

A German antiaircraft gun crew on the top of the Camino mass just before the assault that would eventually dislodge them. These men are most likely members of the 315th Flak Battalion of the 15th Panzer Grenadiers, slated to defend the mass at all costs. These Germans fiercely defended Mt Camino and Difensa during the eight-day campaign. (IWM MH 6320)

FSSF COMMAND STAFF DURING THE DIFENSA CAMPAIGN

Commander - Col Robert T. Frederick
Executive Officer – Lt Col Paul Adams
S1 (Adjutant) – Lt Col Kenneth Wickham
S2 (Intelligence Officer) – Lt Col Robert Burhans
S4 (Supply and Services Officer) – Lt Col O. J. Baldwin
Surgeon – Maj L. D. Besecker
1st Regiment
Commander – Lt Col Alfred Marshal
1st Battalion CO – Lt Col R.W. Becket
2nd Battalion CO – Lt Col Akehurst

2nd Regiment
Commander – Lt Col D. D. Williamson
1st Battalion CO – Lt Col Thomas MacWilliam (KIA)
1st Battalion CO – Maj Walter Gray (KIA)
1st Battalion CO – Maj Edward Thomas
2nd Battalion CO – Lt Col Moore
3rd Regiment
Commander – Lt Col Edwin Walker
1st Battalion CO – Lt Col Thomas Gilday
2nd Battalion CO – Lt Col John Bourne

Pvt Joseph Dauphinais of the 1st Company, 2nd Regiment concurred that "Van [Ausdale] was king among scouts. He was a real mountain man; he could read terrain as you could read a book. He found an excellent route for us to reach the front of the cliff without being detected by the Germans" (Springer, p.70). It was decided that if ropes could be placed, Maj Thomas and Van Ausdale's route would be the best for a stealthy approach. After doing a personal aerial reconnaissance in a Piper Cub, Frederick concurred that the northern approach by rope would provide the greatest surprise. Not only the Germans but also the Allies had considered the northern approach impassable; Frederick hoped the Germans would continue in their doctrine of defending the southern slopes.

Col Frederick realized that attacking Difensa using ropes would eliminate the ability of 1st Regiment to be able to quickly pass through 2nd Regiment and move on to Remetanea. The 2nd Regiment would have to not only seize the Difensa summit, but also carry the attack on to Remetanea. Col Frederick issued 2nd Regiment its marching orders on November 29:

> The Second Regiment will move from present bivouac to the area 973100-973094-967095-968100 where it will remain in concealed bivouac until dark on the night of D-1/D at which time it will advance up Ridge 368 and seize Hill 960 by daybreak on D-Day. Upon capturing Hill 960 the Second Regiment will immediately advance to capture Hill 907. The Second Regiment will continue to occupy Hill 960 and will be prepared to defend against attack from the South. The Second Regiment will assist by fire the attack of the 142nd Infantry on Mt. Maggiore. The Second Regiment will continue to occupy and hold Mt la Difensa – Mt la Remetanea heights until relieved. (Cited by Joyce, p.153)

The attack originally scheduled for November 28 was postponed until December 3 due to rain and cloud cover.

During the day of December 1, last-minute preparations were being made by all of the men in the First Special Service Force. Each regiment had an important role to play and the men prepared for this mission as they had prepared for all missions during training and on Kiska: with a light-hearted

A vivid aerial photograph that puts into perspective the challenging heights of both Mt Camino and Mt Difensa. The First Special Service Force made its assault in the dark, climbing up the rear of the mountain with ropes and attacking the enemy from a direction that was considered completely impassible. The Force arrived at the summit almost exactly where the arrow for Mt Difensa points in the photograph. This photo also features the famous Mt Cassino, the anchor of the Gustav Line. The Camino–Difensa mass made up the outer wall of the Gustav Line and was at times called the Bernhardt Line. All together these mountains made up the Winter Line. (National Archives)

air, but always professional. While the men packed supplies, joked and got in a last-minute game of craps, the Force's chief intelligence officer, Lt Col Robert Burhans, observed the preparations, and later wrote in the official unit history:

> In a Third Regiment hallway an artist was busy with charcoal converting a wall into mural of a man in baggy pants, pockets bulging with ammunition, grenades, rations. Upon the figure he had drawn a packboard that towered high above him and bulked far behind – a load that dwarfed the man and which contained boxes of rations, ammunition, sleeping bag, rifle, machine gun, mortar and battle miscellany ... he wrote over the burdened figure, "Freddy's Freighters – Difensa or Bust." (Burhans, p.98)

The foresight behind this soldier's satirical drawing would be almost visionary, as the men of 3rd Regiment would soon be loaded down and transporting much-needed vital supplies to their comrades on Difensa.

In the afternoon of December 1, the officers of the FSSF waited in the compound of their barracks at Santa Maria for a special address from their Corps Commander, Maj Gen Geoffrey Keyes. Keyes was known to have thought little of the Force, making comments along the lines of its troops being nothing more than "glamour boys" and "overrated glory boys" (Horn and Wyczynski, p. 168). Upon arriving, Keyes continued with his skepticism: "You have been preceded by a great reputation, but you haven't been blooded yet. War isn't Hollywood glamour stuff and men do not die dramatically" (Burhans, p.98). Even though Keyes outwardly questioned the ability of the Force, his decision to use them as the spearhead against the most formidable position facing the II Corps speaks volumes. If he truly doubted their ability, why would he use them to gain his most vital objective?

At dusk, 139th Brigade of the British 46th Division launched its attack towards Calabritto, meeting heavy enemy resistance. Taking the fight into the next day, little ground was gained, but Operation *Raincoat*, already in motion, would proceed as planned.

Equipment and weapons used on Difensa

The First Special Service Force had always had priority when it came to uniforms, weapons, and equipment. It is without question that when the Force arrived in Italy in November 1943, they were some of the best-equipped soldiers in the theater of operations. A secret memo titled *Annex No 1 To Administrative Order No 2* dated November 27, 1943 (below) details exactly what the Force used when it went into combat a few days later on Difensa.

Ironically, the M1943 field coat is not mentioned in this memorandum, but it was most certainly worn during this campaign. The Force was the first unit in the European theater of operations to be issued this field coat. The V-42 knife was also not mentioned, but was indeed carried by the men of the Force. What did make the Force distinct at Difensa were its baggy mountain trousers, airborne jump boots and rucksacks, as T4 Wieneke of the Service Battalion recalls:

> Our pants were big and real baggy, with huge pockets, much baggier than jump pants. They are known as mountain pants. Out boots were wonderful, too – Cochran jump boots. And our rucksack was dandy. With its wood or steel frame, we could load it down. It was large, and it fit well. It was made to fit and you had to have them fit halfway decent to carry the hundred-fifty-pound loads we were carrying. (Springer, p.30)

It should also be noted that the distinctive reversible parkas that symbolized the Force were most likely issued just after the Difensa campaign. Photographic evidence shows them being worn for the Mt Samucro operation starting on December 25, 1943. It was also during this time that they were issued the Arctic overshoes.

The Force was armed for Difensa much like the other American units in II Corps. The majority of the men carried the Caliber .30 M1, also known as the "Garand." The M1 was a gas-operated semiautomatic rifle that fired the .30-06 cartridge. The weapon could chamber eight rounds loaded into a bloc clip, and upon firing the last round, the clip would eject and the bolt would remain open. The weapon weighed roughly nine and a half pounds. Two men from each section would also have an M7 grenade launcher. Officers were authorized to carry the M1A1 carbine with airborne folding stocks. Each section leader, or those who could get their hands on one, carried the Thompson submachine gun, caliber .45. M1A1. The Thompson fired the .45 ACP cartridges at roughly 700 rounds a minute and utilized both 20- and 30-round detachable magazines. The weapon fully loaded weighed roughly 11 pounds. The M1A1 could be fired in both semiautomatic and fully automatic mode, using a selector switch just above the hand grip. The Thompson had a wooden shoulder stock and hand grips.

Each section also had either an M41 Johnson light machine gun or an M1918 Browning Automatic Rifle (BAR). The M1941 Johnson light machine gun was an exclusive weapon used only by the FSSF in Europe. The Johnson was originally purchased in small quantities by the US Marine Corps, which wanted a light yet reliable weapon for its paratroopers.

ANNEX NO 1 TO ADMINISTRATIVE ORDER NO 2

1. The following individual clothing and equipment will be carried to the front by personnel of combat echelon, and applies to both officers and enlisted men.

a. To be worn.

Band, helmet, camouflage

Belt, cartridge, cal. 30, or pistol – as prescribed by T/E

Boots, parachute

Box, match, waterproof

Cap, wool knit

Spoon, M1926

Drawers, wool

Canteen, w/cup, cover, and grate

Gloves, wool o.d., leather palm

Helmet, complete

Handkerchiefs

Insignia, shoulder sleeve, FSSF

Insignia, NCO or Techn.

Knife, mountain

Pockets, magazine, pistol – for personnel armed with pistol

Pockets, magazine, carbine – 3 per officer Combat Echelon, 2 per officer Base Echelon

Package, first aid, w/first aid packet and sulfadiazine

Shirt, wool o.d.

Socks, wool, heavy

Sweater, wool, high neck

Tags, identification, w/tape or necklace

Suspenders, belt, M1936

Trousers, mountain, w/suspenders

Undershirt, wool

b. To be Carried in a blanket roll over shoulder.

1 Shelter Half, w/poles, pins and rope

Bag, sleeping, mountain

c. To be Carried in the Field Bag.

Rations- 1 C

1 D

1 K

Toilet Articles

Poncho

Extra Socks

2. Rucksacks will be packed with a change of underwear and socks, remaining mess gear, remaining toilet articles and left stacked together at the unit storage point in the Base Camp available to the Supply Officer for delivery to advanced units in case the opportunity arises.

3. a. All troops will carry to the Assembly Area on their persons the items enumerated above in paragraph 1 in addition to their normal weapons and ammunition load.

b. The First and Third Regiments will retain the blanket roll with them until otherwise ordered.

c. The Second Regiment will retain the blanket roll with them until the afternoon of D-1, at which time they will be stacked and turned over to carrying parties, to be withdrawn by the carrying parties to the vicinity of the dump area where they will be kept in bulk, awaiting future use by the regiment. In preparing the rolls for withdrawal to the dump area, companies and detachments will make certain to keep their rolls together and carrying parties will make every effort to keep their rolls separated by organization.

d. At any time that blanket rolls are ordered withdrawn to the supply area, regimental commanders will have them placed near the road or trails, sorted or stacked by company, where they may be kept segregated while being handled by supply personnel.

By Order of Colonel FREDERICK:

PAUL D. ADAMS,
Colonel, 1st Sp Sv Force,
Executive. (Cited by Ross, p.100)

NOVEMBER 29, 1943

FSSF attack on Mt Difensa is put back to December 3

The Force, needing the same thing, made a trade with the Marines. The Force would get 125 Johnson machine guns and in return the Marines would receive the new RS explosive that the Force had been using in training. The Johnson light machine gun fired the standard US Army .30-06 round, using a 20-round detachable magazine that fed into the side of the weapon. The weapon could be loaded or topped off either individually or by a stripper clip that fed into the right side of the weapon while the clip was still attached. The Johnson could be fired single shot from the closed bolt or fully automatic from the open bolt. The handgrip had the safety built in below the trigger

WEAPONS BREAKDOWN BY PLATOON

1x M1A1 carbine
21x M1 rifles
2x M1A1 Thompson submachine guns
2x M41 Johnson light machine guns or
M1918 Browning Automatic Rifles
1x M2 60mm mortar

2x M1919A4 machine guns
30x M1911A1 pistols
30x V42 fighting knives
4x M7 rifle grenade launchers
2x M1 bazookas

guard, and the selector switch was just above the handgrip. The weapon weighed 14 pounds fully loaded and had a removable bipod. The weapon had a 400-round-a-minute cyclic rate. The BAR would eventually come in to supplement the Johnson, as the Force only had 125 of them.

Each section also had the M1919A1 Browning light machine gun, and the weapon fired the standard US Army .30-06 cartridge at a cyclic rate of roughly 500 rounds per minute. The weapon was belt fed, weighed 45 pounds with the tripod, and was air-cooled. The weapon was recoil-operated and it fired from the open bolt. The M1919A1 was intended to be used as a mobile support weapon that could be easily carried and set up. The weapon was crewed by two men: the gunner, and the assistant gunner who would load and help feed the weapon. Two other men in the section would also carry ammunition for the weapon. Each section also had access to the M1 bazooka. The bazooka had a 61in. bore, weighed roughly 13 pounds, and fired M6 and M7 antitank rockets. The weapon utilized an electrical firing system that was charged by batteries.

Each platoon had an M2 60mm mortar, which was operated by a four-man team consisting of a gunner, an assistant gunner, and two ammunition men. The weapon broke down into four parts: the tube, base plate, bipod, and the site. The weapon weighed 42 pounds completely assembled and the tube reached 28 inches in length. The weapon fired the high-explosive M49 A2 round, the M302 WP smoke round, and the M83 illumination round.

The Germans defending the Camino mass were predominantly members of the 15th Panzer Grenadiers. The 15th Panzer Grenadiers had been reconstituted twice in their history. Originally, they were formed as the 15th Panzer Division and shipped to Libya as part of the Afrika Korps in February 1941. The bulk of the division was destroyed and forced to surrender in Tunisia on May 12, 1943. Re-formed in Sicily in July 1943 as the Division Sizilien, they were shortly thereafter retitled the 15th Panzer Grenadier Division. During the Difensa campaign the division was made up of the 104th, 115th, and 129th Panzer Grenadier regiments, the 215th Panzer Battalion,

Three Forcemen from 2nd Company, 1st Regiment in walking-out attire photographed in Naples, Italy 1943. These men all proudly wear their jump wings on their M43 field coats. On the left is R. L. Rozier of Manitoba, Canada, who died as a POW. Center is Howard Bell of Ludlow, Massachusetts and on the right Thomas Phillips of Sequin, Texas, who was later awarded the Silver Star for his actions in Southern France commanding 2nd Platoon, 1st Company. Phillips's platoon had to take out a German bunker during the Hyeres landings. Thomas spent 23 years in the Army. (Author's Collection/ FSSFLHG)

Mountain warfare training was one of the key components to the "Plough Force's" training, as the concept of fighting behind the lines in Norway for extended periods of time required it. Even after the operation was canceled, winter and mountain training continued to be vital. This soldier is firing his M1 rifle with the M1905 bayonet fixed. (National Archives)

the Panzer Grenadier Battalion Reggio, the 33rd Panzer Artillery Regiment, the 315th Flak Battalion, the 33rd Reconnaissance Battalion, the 33rd Panzerjäger Battalion, the 33rd Panzer Pioneer Battalion, the 999 Signals Battalion, and the 33rd Divisional Support Troops

Most of these Panzer grenadiers were issued the standard army K98ks bolt-action rifle that fired a 7.92mm round. The rifle had a five-round integral box magazine that was stripper-clip fed. With a sniper scope, this weapon was very accurate and deadly to the Force on Difensa. Each German platoon was issued roughly five MP40s, commonly referred to as "Schmeissers." These were 9mm submachine guns weighing roughly 8 pounds and containing a 32-round box magazine. These weapons were known for their durability and ferocity in close-quarter combat. The weapon that put the most fear into the Forceman on Difensa was the German MG 34 and the later-made MG 42. Issued four to a platoon, the MG 34 and MG 42 were terrifying weapons due to their incredibly high cyclic rate of 900 and 1,200 rounds per minute respectively; the sound was distinct and unforgettable. The MG 34 and MG 42 were air-cooled, belt-fed weapons that fired the 7.92mm round; weighing in at almost 26 pounds, the weapons were still easy to maneuver.

THE RAID

We tore up all letters and left all identification behind except pay-book and dog-tags.
We're all packed and tonight move up to the front, thank goodness, to do our job...
A. W. Ovenden
(Adleman and Walton, p.123)

The jump-off

At 4:00 pm (1600) on December 1, the 2nd Regiment boarded trucks at their barracks at Santa Maria followed by the 1st and 3rd regiments at hourly intervals. The six-by-six transport trucks would take the men to the town of Presenzano, home of the 36th Division command post. The trucks drove quickly over the muddy roads with only the black-out lights to see what was ahead in the distance. The sky lit up with artillery as the cold rain began to pour. Once in Presenzano they met a guide from the 142nd Infantry that would lead the 2nd Regiment to the base of Mt Difensa, and according to Sgt Donald Mackinnon of the 1st Company, 2nd Regiment, "there was a

The view from behind the 36th Division's positions details the northern approach to Mt Difensa (Hill 960) and Mt Remetanea (Hill 907). Camino (Hill 963) can also be seen in the background. It was from this direction that 2nd Regiment of the First Special Service Force made their surprise climb and attack. Mt Maggiore (Hill 630) to the right was the focus of the 142nd Infantry. Note: the town of Mignano can be seen in the foreground. It was roughly from Hill 368 that the 142nd launched their attack. (National Archives)

1600hrs,
DECEMBER 1

2nd Regt then 1st
and 3rd Regts
boards trucks to
move to
Presenzano

menacing feeling about the whole thing" (Springer, p.72). The British 46th Division had launched its diversionary attack against Hill 360 on the far left flank; this push would last through the night.

At roughly 9:00 pm (2100) the men of 2nd Regiment began what was for some the toughest part of the operation, the night march through the mud and icy creek beds to the staging area half way to the crest of Difensa. It was imperative that 2nd Regiment reached the staging area prior to sunrise so that their movements would not be detected by the German observers. Sgt Mackinnon described the ten-mile march as "loaded down with weapons and gear, including our steel frame rucksack, rations, and water bottle ... We were so exhausted with the effort to keep up, clawing sliding our way in the very difficult conditions, that we thought, if we had to go into action when we arrived, we would be useless" (Springer, p.72). Maj Ed Thomas, 1st Battalion, 2nd Regiment's executive officer, concurs: "that was a miserable, miserable trip from where the trucks dropped us off to the assembly area on the side of the mountain ... in the rain, which was the most miserable aspect. It was tougher than the climb up the mountain." T4 Dawson agrees, "that was the most exhausting part of the climb for me" (Springer, p.73). The men of 2nd Regiment would pass through the positions of the 36th Division who had suffered heavy casualties at the hands of the Panzer grenadiers; shouts of "Nice knowing ya, boys ..." (Nadler, p.107) were made as these battle-hardened infantrymen wondered, "Who the hell was this irregular glamour outfit anyway?" (Springer, p.74). They, along with the Germans atop of Difensa, would find out soon enough who this strange North American force that wore a red spearhead on its left sleeves really were.

Passing the bodies of men slain in earlier attacks, the leading elements of 2nd Regiment reached the staging area halfway to the crest of the mountain at roughly 3:00 am (0300), although the end of the column would not arrive until just before sun up. The secrecy of the operation had been maintained, the rain had stopped and the men of 2nd Regiment took cover in the trees and scrub pine halfway up the mountain. 1st Regiment waited in divisional reserve at the base of the mountain, while 3rd Regiment was split; one battalion was in direct support of the 2nd Regiment at the base of the mountain while the other battalion was to be used to carry supplies, equipment and wounded to and from the summit once engaged. All three regiments rested on the day of the 2nd in the warming December sun, waiting for what they knew would be the toughest mission of their lives.

The wait

The men of 2nd Regiment rested secretly in a thin tree-lined bivouac area just a short way up from the base of Difensa and well inside enemy observation at roughly the 400-meter mark. Mortar rounds began to fall at the base of Difensa, but it appeared that 2nd Regiment's concealment was still intact. Col Frederick met with Gen Clark, Brig Gen Wilbur of the 36th Division and Col Lynch of the 142nd Infantry Division in the morning to finalize plans for the night's raid on the summit. The meeting took place at Lynch's CP, where Frederick was informed that the British 46th Division had

2100 hrs,
DECEMBER 1

2nd Regt begins its
10-mile night
march to below Mt
Difensa

succeeded in taking Hill 360, opening the door for the British 56th Division to make its advance on Mt Camino (Hill 963) on Frederick's left flank. The 56th Division would jump off ahead of the 2nd Regiment at 10:00 pm (2200). The clear sky allowed for the air cover to begin bombing the tops of Difensa, Maggiore, and Camino, with the heaviest bombing around the Cassino mass; roughly 500 tons of ordnance was dropped by the end of the day. Fifth Army had also massed its artillery of roughly 925 guns and had directed its fire on to

A look at Mt Camino and Mt Difensa prior to the attacks in early December of 1943. Mt Camino, also referred to as Hill 963, with a monastery on the top is dead center. Difensa, Hill 960, is on the far right. The British 56th Division was responsible for Hill 963, while the men of the FSSF were challenged with Mt Difensa. Looking closely at the foreground, among the shadows, reveals British officers on a reconnaissance exercise to gather intelligence prior to the assaults. (National Archives)

Camino and Difensa (Burhans, p.102). Col Frederick was then informed that 1st Regiment should be moved to the 36th Division reserve area on the south of Ridge 368, which he agreed to reluctantly as he was hoping to use these men as his own reserve.

As the day progressed, the men of 2nd Regiment checked ammo, cleaned weapons, taped grenades on to their equipment, ate cold K-rations, and did what all soldiers do prior to battle, making small talk and nervously joking with one another as these highly trained soldiers were for the most part untested in battle. At 4:00 pm (1600) orders came for the men to start getting ready. 2nd Regiment's commanding officer, Lt Col Williamson, was told by Frederick that there should be no firing of weapons until the attack: "grenades + knives only will be used until 0630 D-Day – fire begins at 0630 hours" (cited by Joyce, p.154). At 4:30 pm (1630) Col Frederick moved out with his staff consisting of Capt O'Neill, Lt Roll, Sgt Grey and scouts Wright, Pulley, and Hill to create a tactical command post on the southern slope of the mountain. Frederick's front line presence and demeanor always inspired confidence and loyalty among his men – they would follow him anywhere.

The opening phase

As dusk fell, the men of the First Special Service Force began to deploy. 1st Regiment moved over to Hill 368 where it would wait as a reserve force for the 36th Infantry Division. 1st Battalion, 3rd Regiment moved out to the 600-meter assembly area to act as a reserve for 2nd Regiment, while the 2nd Battalion, 3rd Regiment and the Service Battalion prepared to move ammunition and supplies and act as stretcher bearers and medics. 2nd Regiment began its arduous assent up the mountain in single-file columns, passing the Allied bodies from previously failed attacks that were unable to be retrieved. It was at this time, 4:30 pm (1630), that the Fifth Army began what Chief Intelligence Officer Lt Col Burhans has described as "the heaviest concentration of artillery in the Italian campaign thus far,

DAYTIME, DECEMBER 2

2nd Regiment waits in a thin tree-lined bivouac area just above base of Mt Difensa

25-pdr guns of the 146th Field Regiment, Royal Artillery, hammer away at the Camino mass. Even with such a heavy concentration of artillery, the effects were minimal against the Germans dug in on Difensa and Camino. (IWM NA 9299)

perhaps the heaviest in the war." Roughly all 925 artillery pieces belonging to the Fifth Army opened fire along the entire front. The noise was deafening and the scene was menacing, as high explosives coupled with white phosphorus made for an ominous start to a very long night. The barrage was intended to soften the enemy positions on Mt Difensa and the rest of the Camino mass. Mt Difensa would soon be nicknamed the "Million Dollar Mountain" by many of the Force, based on the estimated price of the bombardment.

Supporting artillery began to increase its range to cover the secondary objectives while the German 105mm, 155mm, and 170mm guns answered back. The Germans knew every path, trail, and defensive position leading up to the summit of Difensa, and they demonstrated this to the Forcemen using mortar rounds and sniper fire. Rounds fell on the trails, the supply areas, the command post, and even the aid station.

By 10:30 pm (2230) the 2nd Regiment had reached the base of the northeastern side of the cliff just below the summit plateau. Four men were given the duty of taking the ropes up the cliff. Canadian Scout Sgt Thomas Fenton and American Scout S/Sgt Howard Van Ausdale were tasked with the arduous duty of scouting out the most passable approach to the top of Mt Difensa. Climbing the cliffs as stealthily as possible in pitch darkness, using only their hands and legs in the bitter cold, the men reached the summit. Eluding a German sentry, the men tied off the ropes for their comrades. Behind Fenton and Ausdale were Pvt Joseph Dauphinais and Sgt John Walter with the two ropes that would be tied to the scout's ropes. With the ropes secured, the 1st Battalion, 2nd Regiment waited for orders to proceed into what would be for most their first combat experience against battle-hardened Panzer grenadiers.

The success of the operation depended on first getting 2nd Regiment to the top of the mountain without being detected and secondly keeping them supplied once there. Lt Col Tom MacWilliam's 1st Battalion consisting of 1st Company under Lt C. W. Rothlin, 2nd Company under Capt Stan Waters,

On the eastern slopes of Mt Difensa smoke and HE rounds can be seen impacting the side of the mountain. This photograph was most likely taken prior to the main attack on December 3, as the Allies did everything they could to soften the position prior to the raid. (National Archives)

and 3rd Company under Capt Daugherty would lead the assault, going up the ropes with just weapons, ammunition, and musette bags. Once on top, 1st Company would take the left flank, 2nd Company the center, and 3rd Company would take the right flank. Forming a skirmish line of sorts, they would advance on the enemy positions from the rear. The 2nd Battalion of the 2nd Regiment under Lt Col Bob Moore would follow up directly in reserve, carrying the extra equipment, weapons, ammunition, and water up the ropes. Once the plateau of Difensa was supposedly secured, 3rd Regiment would follow up with an endless human supply train of ammunition, food, water, medical supplies, and blankets.

The climb

At roughly 1:00 am (0100) on December 3, 2nd Regiment, 1st Battalion was ordered by Col Frederick to proceed up the ropes to the summit of Mt Difensa. The journey to the top would be slow, allowing only two men to go at a time as there were only two ropes attached to the peak. Climbing a roughly 70-degree incline forced the men to expend a lot of energy as they had to grip the ropes and mountain crevices in the pitch darkness. The weight of the weapons, ammunition and equipment strained every muscle, while the stress of being as stealthy as possible went through everyone's

The climb (overleaf)

At roughly 1:00 am (0100) on the night of December 2–3, 1943, the men of 1st Battalion, 2nd Regiment made their infamous climb to the summit of Mt Difensa. Using only two ropes, the men stealthily climbed to the summit of the mountain undetected by the German garrison at the top. "The difficulty of the climb with combat loads was compounded by the dark night and the wet, treacherous terrain. Scrambling in the dark up the rocky trail with every foot and handhold doubtful demanded superhuman effort by the men loaded with

weapons, ammunition, radios, and litters. To our ears every rock displaced clattered downhill with sound magnified a thousand times and raised the question in our minds, 'did the enemy hear this?', a not very comforting thought." (Horn and Wyczynski, p.174) The ropes were strategically placed by Canadian Scout Sgt Thomas Fenton and American Scout S/Sgt Howard Van Ausdale. The 1st Battalion deployed by companies, with 1st Company in the lead followed by 2nd and 3rd companies. All three companies were able to reach the summit without being detected, a truly remarkable feat.

mind, as one false step by one Forceman could blow the entire operation. As the cold rain fell, one by one, each man made his way over the lip of the cliff wall on to the summit. The artillery barrage started shifting westward overhead towards the secondary target of Mt Remetanea, thus providing a covering echo so that the men's movement could be somewhat concealed; however, discretion and noise discipline was still critical for the success of the raid. Sgt Walter Lewis of 1st Company recalls:

I had quite a load on me. I was carrying rifle grenades and an M1 rifle. Damnit, I had a hell of a time climbing that mountain and had a rough time when I got to the ropes. It was the last section of line and I kept spinning and swinging around and around because of the weight I was carrying. It was a rough climb for me. (Springer, p.77)

Mountain climbing would become an essential component of a Forceman's training while at Ft Harrison. This particular part of the training is what made the climb at Mt Difensa possible and is what set the Force aside from other specially trained commando units. "We trained on rock faces, going up and rappelling back down." (Springer, p.27) (National Archives)

Struggling in the rainy cold pitch darkness of the climb, many of the men were relieved to just make the summit in one piece and without giving up the entire operation. Once on the summit, the men broke right and left around the plateau, slowly moving into position and waiting for the rest of the company to arrive. It was dark, wet, and cold, with heavy fog making visibility almost zero. All they could do was wait and remain quiet.

At roughly 3:00 am (0300), 1st Company was completely over the top and forming ad hoc skirmish lines. Slowly they moved forward behind the enemy machine gun positions, pressing the left flank. By roughly 4:30 am (0430), 2nd Company was completely off the ropes and moving into position down the center. Even though contact had been lost with 1st Company, 3rd Company continued up the ropes, forming up at the summit for their planned push on the right flank. The element of surprise had been achieved, as Don Mackinnon of 1st Company recalled:

We reached the top without challenge. The Germans had not set up defensive positions above the cliffs assuming that this approach was unassailable ... Once on top we started along a narrow rough and rocky path toward the German positions concentrated in a saucer-like area ahead of us. It seemed quieter now as we tried to make as little noise as possible. Second and third platoons were close behind us on the path. The whole company had reached the top without detection. We had got further than any earlier assaults and had achieved the element of surprise. (Cited by Horn and Wyczynski, p.175)

Fifth Army artillery continued to pound Mt Remetanea, and the shells passed over the heads of the veiled soldiers of the FSSF on top of Mt Difensa. The noise was deafening, yet welcomed by the men that were relying on it to cover their movement.

Members of the 1st London Scottish Regiment, 56th Division, X Corps, work their way up the rocky slopes of Camino. This photograph demonstrates the almost impossible task that the British faced. Unlike the First Special Service Force, which was able to approach the summit of Difensa using ropes from the cliff face at the rear of the German positions, the British did not have the same option. Having to assault Hill 963 from its base, the British suffered extremely high causalities. (IWM NA 9630)

The attack

3rd Platoon, 1st Company, the lead element of the assault, stealthily inched towards the German positions when an enemy sentry happened upon S/Sgt Van Ausdale, who immediately killed the sentry with his knife. Sgt Waling of 1st Company recalls: "One of the scouts nailed one of those of German sentries, who rolled down the cliff and landed right beside and below me. He was gasping for air." (Springer, p 78). Just feet away from the German positions, still undetected, the morning silence would soon be shattered.

At roughly 5:30am (0530), two hours ahead of schedule, loose rocks being kicked in the darkness or, as some claim, a helmet falling off from a soldier's head alerted the Panzer grenadiers to the presence of the 2nd Regiment. Sgt Mackinnon of 1st Company recalls, "We were virtually on top of the German positions when someone kicked a rock loose and a German challenged the two scouts. Someone shot, and that's when machinegun fire opened up all around us" (Springer, p.78). Seizing the element of surprise, Capt. Rothlin's 1st Company engaged the enemy in bitter close combat. Flares illuminated the early morning sky while machinegun and mortar fire poured into the men of 2nd Regiment. Sgt Glass of 1st Company recalls:

The attack begins (overleaf)

At roughly 5:30 am (0530), 1st Company, 1st Battalion, 2nd Regiment began the attack on the German defenders on the peak of Mt Difensa, following the sounds of falling rocks or a helmet that had alerted the Panzer Grenadiers to their presence. "We got into it right away ... we were at their back door, and they were surprised ... We had fixed our bayonets ... because we were working real close ... in no time at all, I didn't have a grenade left ... I threw them at everybody." "Stuff was really flying around there. The German fire was pretty heavy, but I don't think they knew what they were shooting at or really believed what was happening." (Springer, pp.79– 80) The fighting was vicious, close-quarter hand-to-hand-style combat. After about an hour the Force held the summit, allowing 2nd Battalion, 2nd Regiment to reach the top and consolidate the newly acquired positions. German resistance remained heavy as the Force had yet to take the entire mountain mass of Mt Remetanea.

A German mortar team in an unknown defensive position somewhere in Italy, 1944. These soldiers man the 8cm Granatwerfer Model 34, caliber 81mm, originally designated as the heavy mortar until the 120mm was introduced. This was the standard mortar of the German infantry throughout the war. Mortars like this were used on Mt Difensa and were incredibly troublesome to the Forcemen. With paths and trails already zeroed in, the Germans were able to dispense countless rounds on the unsuspecting Forcemen. The Germans also used tracer rounds from machine guns to mark the targets for their mortarmen. (Bundesarchiv, Bild 101I-316-1190-27, photo: o.Ang)

We got into it right away. Of course, we were at their back door, and they were surprised, so we got in a lot of time before they even knew what was happening. We had fixed our bayonets because we had anticipated hand to hand combat, and thank God we did, because we were working real close. It was pretty hectic and I'm not sure what happened those first few seconds. But in no time at all, I didn't have a grenade left. I really used them to good advantage. I threw them at everybody. There was a Kraut down below me over a ledge shooting tracers straight up in the air. I just dropped one right down on his head. They're good weapons, if you know how to use them. (Springer, p.79–80)

Pvt Dauphinais of 1st Company recalls, "Stuff was really flying around there. The German fire was pretty heavy, but I don't think they knew what they were shooting at or really believed what was happening. Maybe they couldn't believe we were that audacious. How could anybody come in your back door?" (Springer, p.80). The initial assault was chaotic as the battle-hardened Panzer grenadiers fought back savagely, making the Forcemen pay for every yard of ground on top of Mt Difensa. Pvt Betts of 1st Company recalls:

We got our machine gun activated and turned it loose on anything that remotely resembled a Kraut. It seemed like it didn't take long to run out of ammo. I grabbed a rifle from one of the guys who was lying there dead, and I advanced. I think it was because I was scared and very, very busy that I don't really remember too much of what happened that first few minutes. I don't think anyone really knew what was going on. (Springer, p.80)

The six German MG 42 machinegun emplacements that had covered the northern approaches to the summit, dug in and untouched by the previous artillery barrage, had by now turned on their attackers from the rear. The Germans had been caught by surprise and this allowed for 2nd Regiment to gain a solid grip around the northern rim of the saucer.

Lt Col MacWilliam of 2nd Regiment directed the assault from a forward shell hole with the advanced platoon. MacWilliam started to pinpoint the enemy strongholds and directed the FSSF men to target them with their own mortars and machine guns. 1st Company was taking heavy casualties, as Pvt Dauphinais states:

There were fire fights on both sides of my position ... The Krauts were so close I could have spit in the bugger's eye. Three of them worked on me for a while there. They were

putting out a lot of lead … It was a
terrible weapon [MG 42] I could see
the muzzle flashes blinking at me, but
there wasn't much I could do at the
time. I never saw so many flashes in my
life … I was pinned down in the open
and it was only a matter of time, really.
I didn't have a chance. They plugged
me. I don't know if it was the shock of
the bullet hitting me or what, but I
passed out. (Springer, p.81–82)

The last German strongholds on
the summit were the dug-in MG 42
nests that were causing serious
casualties among the Forcemen.
Sgt McGinty's section was trying to take out one of the positions as they had
become pinned down and were taking casualties. S/Sgt Van Ausdale and
Sgt Fenton, the scouts who had attached the ropes and led the assault, gave
crucial support:

Private Johnson of the 1st London Scottish Regiment makes his way up the slopes of Mt Camino. The British in X Corps, 56th Division had an extremely difficult fight for the control of Camino. On several occasion they were repulsed by ferocious counterattacks made by the stubborn German defenders. Without the British taking Camino, the gains made by the First Special Service Force on Difensa would have been ineffectual. (IWM NA 9632)

> [They] saw the section's position and swung to the left flank where they both delivered
> automatic fire on the enemy until the McGinty section could remove its wounded …
> Sergeant Van Ausdale gathered up eight such men, ordered a nearby machinegun team
> to lay down fire, called for three mortar rounds from the company emplacement and
> led his improvised section over the ledge in a straight assault on the first cave. Grenades
> and bayonets got the first cave and the same instruments dispatched the second gun
> further up. (Burhans, p.106)

Lt Col MacWilliam ordered Captain Rothlin's 1st Company and Water's
2nd Company to take out the remaining the gun emplacements. 3rd Platoon,
1st Company would lay down suppressing fire while the rest of 1st and 2nd
companies would flank the remaining guns. Lt Kaasch's platoon formed a
skirmish line: "taking two men he [Lt Kaasch] advanced on the guns. Caught
on the flank the first gun crew surrendered intact; similar tactics caught the
second gun crew still firing where a few grenades effectually silenced the
gun. Few enemy were found alive" (Burhans, p.106). The remaining pockets
of Germans began to surrender, white flags appeared from behind rocks and
fighting positions, while many other Panzer grenadiers made a hasty
withdrawal across the saddle to Mt Remetanea. German soldiers were seen
surrendering all over the summit, but some grenadiers continued to resist
and refused to surrender, causing one of the most controversial moments
during the fight for Mt Difensa.

As Germans were surrendering, Capt Rothlin was reported to be taking
in a group of prisoners with a white flag, when in close proximity a German
prisoner produced a gun and shot Rothlin in the face. Another account
indicates that Capt Rothlin, who was moving forward to assess the enemy

situation, looked up from behind the cover of a rock and was shot in the head by a German soldier with a Schmeisser who had not yet surrendered. Yet another account indicates that Rothlin and Forceman Syd Gath stood up from behind a rock to cover a couple of Germans who had their hands up in an attempt to surrender and were both shot in the head by an MP 40. Whether Rothlin was or was not shot by a German who was surrendering may never be truly known. What is known is that the mountain top was a chaotic scene; some Germans were surrendering while others continued to fight on. Sniper rounds from Mt Remetanea continued to hit their targets and mortar rounds fell everywhere.

The rumor of Rothlin's death was apparently enough for some members of the FSSF to have a "take no prisoners" mentality, as Sgt Stonehouse stated: "Some of the guys were shooting German prisoners, but hey that's the way it was. They were the enemy … and we lost a lot of good buddies up there, and tempers were pretty hot" (Springer, p.88). Other reports indicate that Capt Rothlin was not the only Forceman potentially tricked by surrendering Germans. One account indicated that the Germans walked towards the Forcemen, appearing to surrender, yet behind their backs they concealed their machine pistols and once in close range they would bring them round and fire on the unsuspecting commandos. The Forcemen learned quickly and would order advancing Germans to halt: if this order was ignored, they were shot. After Rothlin's death, 1st Lt Larry Piette was now in command of 1st Company. In the confusion of close-quarter combat the men began to bunch up. With the fighting still intense, Piette ordered his men to spread out and clear the rest of the summit. Lt Col MacWilliam ordered his men of 1st Battalion to start to consolidate their newly won positions against what he feared would be a strong German counterattack. MacWilliam's men were covering the approach from the south and from the west, where Mt Remetanea still remained very active with German resistance.

A German soldier of an unknown unit in Italy operates the dreaded MG 34. With a cyclic rate of 800 to 900 rounds per minute, the MG 34 roared with a very distinct and chilling sound. Many of the positions on Mt Difensa were defended with these weapons, which were easy to turn around; they quickly went to work on the Forcemen, who had caught the Germans by surprise. (Bundesarchiv, Bild 101I-575-1808-04, photo: Erwin Seeger)

By 7:00 am (0700) all of 1st Battalion was on the summit and 2nd Battalion under Lt Col Moore was starting to arrive in force to the right of the 1st Battalion. A forward artillery observer reported, "Capt Fielding to CO, FSSF: Ln O, 27th & 68th reports Lt. Col. Moore has consolidated first obj after clearing up earlier resistance. Lt. Col. MacWilliam is just short of 2nd Obj and moving up" (cited by Joyce, p.157). 2nd Battalion began to move into 1st Battalion's positions as part of the planned relief effort, allowing MacWilliam to reorganize his battered forces for the push on Remetanea (Hill 907), where he already had reconnaissance patrols probing westward. Low on ammunition, the ranks depleted with casualties, exhausted from the climb and the two straight hours of close-quarter combat on the summit, the men of 1st Battalion formed into columns for the assault on Hill 907. Lt Col MacWilliam wanted to take Remetanea before the Germans had a chance to regroup and organize a solid defense. The 142nd Infantry Regiment of the 36th Division had secured Hill 370 while the FSSF had been taking Difensa, and was now working its way up to the main ridge leading towards Mt Maggiore. The 142nd would not be able to hold Maggiore unless Remetanea was in Allied hands. MacWilliam, realizing this, mobilized his men for the attack.

Mortars, artillery, and snipers were the threat of the morning as the Germans had marked pre-existing targets on Difensa and the surrounding ridgelines. Artillery rained down on the men of 2nd Regiment, making them feel exposed and vulnerable to the unseen enemy. MacWilliam, the New Brunswick history professor, following the First Special Service Force maxim of commanding from the front, was going personally to lead the attack along the ridgeline heading to Remetanea. In front of the first company he gave the order to move out. Just then, a mortar round landed on to the battalion staff, instantly killing MacWilliam and two others and wounding the rest. MacWilliam's citation reads:

> The 1st Battalion 2nd Regiment, commanded by Lt.-Col. T.C. MacWilliam, was the assault Bn. and led the attack up the mountainside. Lt.-Col. MacWilliam accompanying the advanced platoon of 1st Company, directed the attack through a heavy firefight and took the mountain peak with one Company, and from his advance position directed the attack on the remaining enemy positions. By this time his Battalion was disorganized, since 2nd Company had lost contact on the way up and 1st Company had suffered severe losses. The position was subjected to heavy mortar and sniper fire. Despite all this Lt.-Col. MacWilliam went about calmly consolidating his position

Sgt Harold "Ted" Johnson of 4th Company, 2nd Regiment is photographed in Canadian battledress after the breakup of the Force. Sgt Johnson was born in St Paul, Minnesota, and joined the Canadian Army on June 20, 1941, months before the attack on Pearl Harbor. While in training he answered the call for a special unit that would turn out to be the First Special Service Force. Ironically, Ted Johnson was an American in the Canadian Army now serving in an integrated American–Canadian unit supplied and equipped by the United States. As a member of 2nd Regiment, Johnson was wounded on Mt Difensa. He was able to rejoin his unit just prior to Anzio, serving with the Force until its breakup in December 1944. Following the breakup, Johnson returned to Canadian service, in which he was stationed in England as training staff and then discharged in 1946. (The Johnson Family)

0700 hrs, DECEMBER 3

All of 1st Bn is on the summit and the objective secured, 2nd Bn follows

against possible counter attack encouraging his men and always planning the next attack. (Cited by Joyce, p.157–58)

With the command group killed or wounded, the assault stalled. Maj Ed Thomas, 1st Battalion, 2nd Regiment's executive officer, realizing that his friend Lt Col MacWilliam had been killed, assumed command and prepared to push the attack forward. Col Frederick, who had made his command post at the base of the rope area, had now ascended to the summit to assess the situation (due to radio failure). Linking up with Maj Thomas, Frederick ordered 2nd Regiment to consolidate their positions and hold the attack until ammunition and reinforcements could be brought forward. Capt O'Neill remembered, "With bullets raking the air, Frederick moved from unit to unit, sending out patrols and placing men in outposts, to gradually widen the piece of territory we held" (cited by Horn and Wyczynski, p.179).

Officers of the Force always led their men from the front, and no one perpetuated this more readily than Col Frederick himself. Capt O'Neill observed, "Perhaps we lost more officers than we should, as they needlessly exposed themselves … His [Col Frederick's] indifference to enemy fire was hard to explain, as there were times when a heavy barrage of mortar fire would send us scurrying for cover only to come back and find him smoking a cigarette – in the same position and place we had vacated in hurry" (cited by Adleman and Walton, p.133). Force Scout Sgt Gray remembers, "no matter how far ahead I got, the colonel was always farther. He was always closer to being shot than anybody" (cited by Horn and Wyczynski, p.179).

The fight for the control of the summit was intense and very personal, bringing the American and Canadian Forcemen face to face with the

A machine-gun crew of the Cheshire Regiment on the summit of Mt Camino. Notice the use of rain capes: both the British and the Forceman had to deal with freezing December rains on the Camino mass, making an already difficult task even more miserable. After several attempts, finally the British were able to seize and hold the summit of Mt Camino on December 6. On December 7, the British soldiers and members of the Force linked up in the saddle area between Camino and Difensa. (IWM NA 9375)

German Panzer grenadiers. For most of the men of the FSSF this was their first fight, but the battle-hardened defenders would not have been able to ascertain that based on the tactical skill and ferocity of the attackers. The attack worked because of the intense training the Forcemen had received. The tactic of speed and intense firepower overwhelmed the German defenders. Each Forceman was in peak physical shape, allowing them to master the difficult terrain quickly, stealthily, and masterfully. They were also well-trained marksmen and hand-to-hand combat experts. The intense training that each Forceman had undergone also created a very strong mental attitude towards combat, an attitude that they were among the best soldiers in the world and that no enemy was superior.

At 8:35 am (0835) on December 3, Col Frederick received word from the British liaison officer that hills 727, 819, and 963 (Mt Camino) had been taken by the British 169th Brigade. This report was only partially true, as the Germans still held the northwestern face of Camino and used the heights to direct fire on to Difensa.

A typical German solider of an unknown unit in Italy, February 1944. He is most likely a Panzer grenadier somewhere on the Winter Line. These seasoned veterans were able to hold up the Fifth Army for months on its attempted drive to Rome. It was soldiers like this that the First Special Service Force were able to surprise on the early morning of December 3 as they climbed behind the Germans' defensive positions and attacked from the peak. (Bundesarchiv, Bild 101I-310-0864-08A, photo: Engel)

2nd Regiment could not move forward on to Remetanea until it was resupplied, so their only option was to wait it out under heavy mortar, artillery, and sniper fire, as the casualty rates continued to climb. The Germans began to reinforce the saddle area between Difensa and Camino while still holding Mt Remetanea. The situation was becoming dire.

By 11:00 am (1100) the 142nd Infantry Regiment had taken Hill 59. Brig Gen Wilbur of the 36th Division was becoming impatient with the situation and wanted Remetanea (Hill 907) neutralized so that he could press the attack on Mt Maggiore. Tired of waiting for the FSSF to capture 907, Wilbur pushed on to Mt Maggiore anyway with the 142nd at roughly 2:30 pm (1430). Too late in the day to launch an attack, Frederick sent the following message to 2nd Regiment's commander Col Williamson and Maj Gray at roughly 3:30 pm (1530):

> Understand you will attack 907 at daylight 4 Dec. Through your forward Arty Observers call for such fire on positions to your W as needed to keep enemy pinned down during tonight and in preparation for your atk. Great concern felt over area to your South. We are responsible for area South to saddle between LA DIFENSA and CAMINO. Have strong patrols cover area tonight to eliminate opposition to friendly trps S of you and protect your S. flank from atk during night and your atk on 907 in the morning. Keep me informed of developments. Use Arty to full advantage. Deeply regret sad report on MacWilliam. (Cited by Joyce, p.159)

The spearhead of 3rd Regiment's resupply effort had started to arrive on the summit, bringing word that the British had lost the monastery on Camino after a fierce counterattack that morning.

OPERATION *RAINCOAT*

DECEMBER 3–9, 1943

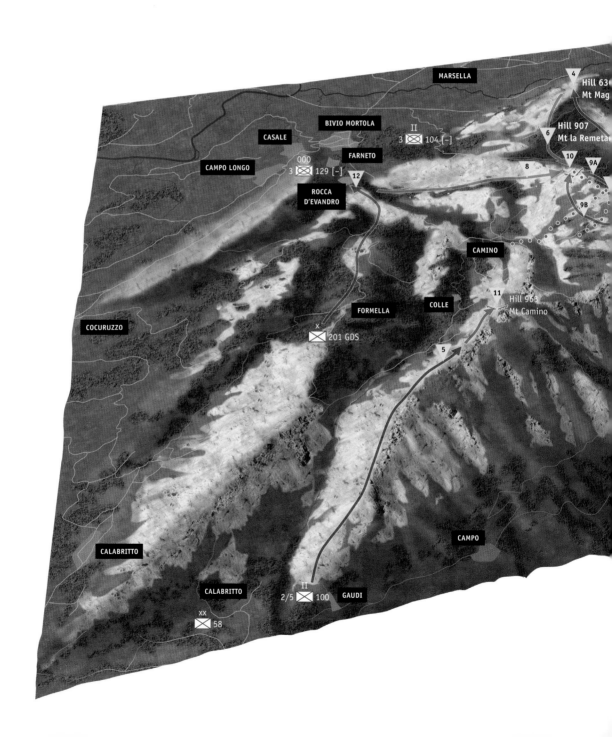

MARSELLA

4 Hill 63
Mt Mag

BIVIO MORTOLA

Hill 907
Mt la Remeta

CASALE

II
3 ⊠ 104 [–]

6

CAMPO LONGO

FARNETO

10
9A

000
3 ⊠ 129 [–]

8

12

ROCCA
D'EVANDRO

9B

CAMINO

COLLE

11
Hill 963
Mt Camino

FORMELLA

COCURUZZO

x
⊠ 201 GDS

5

CALABRITTO

CAMPO

CALABRITTO

II
2/5 ⊠ 100

GAUDI

xx
⊠ 58

EVENTS

1. Night of December 2/3: 2nd Regiment FSSF makes the climb to the summit

2. 0420hrs, December 3: 2nd Regiment FSSF takes Mt La Difensa

3. 0945hrs December 3: 2nd Regiment FSSF probes the approaches to Hill 907

4. 0700–1700hrs December 3: 142nd Infantry Regiment takes Mt Maggiore

5. December 2–3: British 169th Brigade secures a portion of Mt Camino

6. December 4: German troops reinforce the Mt La Remetanea area

7. December 4: pockets of strong German resistance

8. 0335hrs, December 5: Germans mass for a counterattack

9a. 1300 December 5: 1st Battalion, 2nd Regiment FSSF fights its way up the La Remetanea saddle

9b. 1630 December 5: 2nd Battalion, 2nd Regiment and 2nd Company, 1st Regiment attack the knobs on the Difensa/Camino saddle

10. December 6: At first light 1st Battalion, 2nd Regiment seizes Mt La Remetanea

11. December 6: British 169th Brigade takes Mt Camino

12. December 9: British 201st Guards takes Rocca D'Evandro

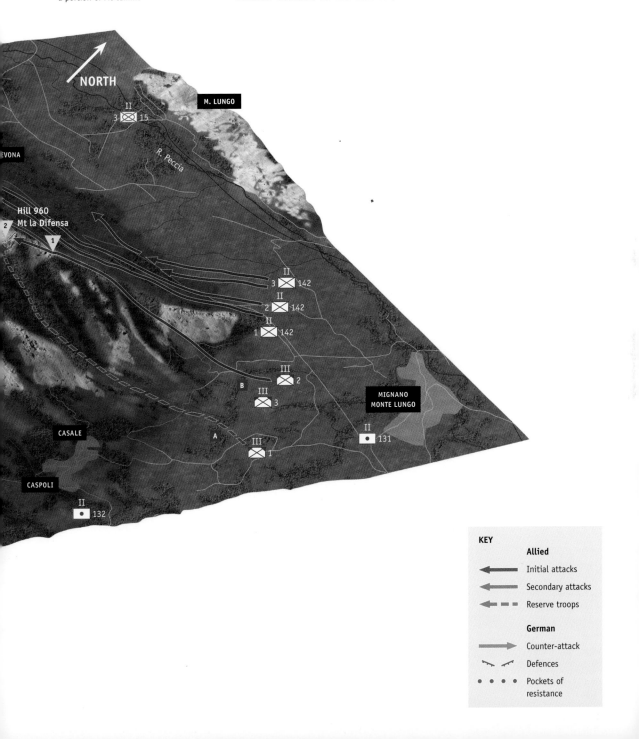

KEY

Allied

← Initial attacks

← Secondary attacks

←- - - Reserve troops

German

→ Counter-attack

⌐⌐ Defences

• • • • Pockets of resistance

The resupply

By 5:00 pm (1700) 3rd Regiment started to arrive with the much-needed resupplies and stretchers for the wounded. The supply effort for Difensa was a logistical nightmare that would have stalled or ended most attacks. Vehicles and mules were out of the question; the only way to bring the vital supplies and stretchers to the summit of Difensa was solely through the men of the 3rd Regiment and the Service Battalion. Under direct enemy mortar, artillery, and sniper fire, the men of 3rd Regiment made the eight-hour treks up to the summit loaded down with pack boards full of ammunition, blankets, food, and other needed supplies while also carrying jerry cans filled with water. On the way down, they carried their wounded comrades to the aid stations. John Bourne commented:

> At first, the men felt that this was not what they had been trained to do and, in fact, were a little insulted. Their attitude changed, however, when they found that ordinary supply troops or medical orderlies would never have been able to withstand the rigors and hardships involved when battling that mountain. As an example, it took eight men about ten hours using mountain climbing ropes, etc., to bring a wounded man down from the top of the mountain to a point where he could be placed on an ambulance jeep. (Adleman and Walton, p.134)

A strange supply request was ordered by Col Frederick that day for whiskey and condoms to be sent to the men on the summit. It is reported that the quartermaster general wondered if the men of 2nd Regiment were having a party on Difensa. The reality is the men on top did not have blankets or shelter halves, only ponchos. The whiskey was requested to warm them up a bit and offer brief comfort in a difficult situation. The condoms were used to keep the men's weapons dry, a trick they leaned in the Aleutians. When Gen Clark heard of the request, he was reported as saying something along the lines of "they took the mountain, give them what they want." By the end

Mules of the 157th Pack Train move through the Pozzilli Valley. In many cases mules could go where jeeps and trucks could not. Many soldiers in the Fifth Army were supplied exclusively with mules. The FSSF on Difensa did not share this luxury, having to rely on the soldiers themselves as the pack mules, as the men of the 3rd Regiment can testify. (National Archives)

Members of the 3rd Regiment pass a mule relay point in the Cervaro sector on January 14, 1944. Forcemen would commonly change from combat to support roles depending on the mission. These men of 3rd Regiment had dropped their weapons to act as stretcher-bearers and human mules on Difensa just over a month prior to this photograph being taken. The nickname given to 3rd Regiment was "Freddie's Freighters" and is certainly understandable, given the amount of supplies and materials these men had to carry on their own backs. The scene was slightly different on Difensa, as the trails were much narrower and they had to use the ropes to reach the summit. (National Archives)

of the day, most of 3rd Regiment was involved with the resupply effort. 1st Battalion had been held in reserve for 2nd Regiment, but was now bringing up supplies. 2nd and 4th companies acted as stretcher bearers, 3rd, 5th and 6th companies were carrying supplies, while 1st Company was ordered to reinforce the top. The battle to resupply the summit was deadly and exhausting; a 3rd Company sergeant recalled, "This operation was the worst for fatigue … We got quite a bit of sniper fire … we … ran into mortar fire that blew legs off and did much damage" (Cited by Joyce, p.160). Another 3rd Regiment man commented, "the Germans were applying a sweeping fire from one end of the trail and then swept back. As they were pounding the trail, they were also bombing both ends of it to cut off escape routes. Their shells and bombs were being guided by snipers who were firing tracers to direct their fire" (Horn and Wyczynski, p.181).

Throughout the day, Lt Roll, Frederick's intelligence officer, was busy interrogating the 43 German prisoners captured that day. He discovered that Difensa was the extreme left flank of the 15th Panzer Grenadier Division:

> It had been the strongpoint of the Winter Line held by the 3d Battalion, 104 Panzer Grenadier Regiment: two companies on Difensa proper holding the caves and bunkers, two more companies strung along the 960–963 ridge line stretching across the saddle on the south. Another two companies of the 115th Reconnaissance Battalion had gone up two days earlier to reinforce Difensa against the imminent attack and it was these troops the Force injured most. (Burhans, p.108)

Roll had determined that roughly a battalion of Germans had retreated to the south or to Hill 907, thus making the perception of a counterattack imminent, but as the day dragged on this counterattack failed to develop. A total of 75 German dead were counted on top of Difensa on December 3.

"Freddie's Freighters" (opposite)

The men of 3rd Regiment and the Service Battalion were tasked with the arduous duty of resupplying the men on top of Mt Difensa. Climbing up steep narrow mountain paths where no animal could go, these men carried food, water, ammunition, medical supplies, and heavy weapons while being sniped at and mortared the entire time. On their return trips down the mountain they acted as stretcher-bearers, bringing back their wounded comrades. "We began carrying the supplies up after the initial battle was finishing above. It was pretty tough … During this period, we were being shelled with mortars. The shelling never seemed to stop. It was one of those deals where one round hit below us and another hit above us and, all of a sudden, it hits you" (Springer, p.99). Without the superhuman effort of these men in support, the 2nd Regiment would not have been able to carry out its mission on top of Difensa, thus jeopardizing the whole campaign. 3rd Regiment would nickname themselves Freddie's Freighters for their role in the battle of Mt Difensa.

Not all of the German prisoners went down the hill after being captured; one Panzer grenadier medic chose to stay on the mountain and help with the Allied wounded. A Forceman with a chest wound was in critical condition and the Allied medics were not sure what to do. The German medic stopped a sucking chest wound and promptly saved the man's life. Forcemen would remember this German medic fondly, as many owed their life to him. His fate after Difensa is unknown, but many had hoped to thank him one day. The FSSF suffered roughly 20 killed and 160 wounded in just the first few hours of fighting, but as the day wore on the casualties continued to mount.

By 9:00 pm (2100) the men of 2nd Regiment were settling in for an uncomfortable and tense night on the top of Mt Difensa. The fog had turned into rain, so that 2nd Regiment now had to battle the cold and wet conditions of the mountain. Fatigue from the previous night and day's fighting had many worn down and numb. There were no shelter halves and just a few blankets, so the men had to remain vigilant while waiting for a possible counterattack. Enemy fire remained constant throughout the night, and rain and fog made the situation almost unbearable. 2nd Regiment patrols were sent out throughout the night to ascertain enemy troop strengths and positions.

1st Regiment, under the command of Col Marshall, was still being held as the 36th Division's reserve force. Spending the day in relative ease, barring the occasional artillery and mortar round, they would now find themselves in the thick of the Mt Difensa quagmire. German artillery began to rain down on 1st Regiment's location, pushing the men out of their positions so they were forced to move westward away from their trail. At roughly 11:00 pm (2300) Gen Wilbur of the 36th Division released Lt Col Becket's 1st Battalion to reinforce the men at the top of Hill 960. Almost immediately upon moving out German observers spotted them; snipers firing tracer rounds marked their positions on the trails and this was followed by an intense artillery barrage. 2nd Battalion would also be spotted by German artillery observers, and over the next 20 minutes 1st Regiment would be pounded by "High-Explosive, air-burst, dead-head armor-piercing, white phosphorus – every type of round in the stockpile … Without knowing what he had hit the enemy had rendered First Regiment, which had not yet struck a blow, exactly forty per cent ineffective" (Burhans, p.111–12). As the rolling barrage moved up the trail, 1st Battalion regrouped and moved on to reinforce the men on Difensa, while 2nd Battalion cared for the casualties and bivouacked for the night. The 2nd Canadian Parachute Battalion War Diary

1700 hrs, DECEMBER 3

3rd Regt arrives at summit with supplies and stretchers

briefly summarized the day: "Reports from the front advise that the 2nd Regiment took their objectives one and one half hours ahead of schedule but lost one hill during a counter attack during the day. Casualties are fairly high" (cited by Wood, p.202).

3rd Regiment would continue its round-the-clock resupply of the men on top of Difensa, braving the cold, rain, snipers, and mortars while acting as human mules for the benefit of their brothers on top. This would be a hellish night for all of the men of the First Special Service Force, and all three regiments were now baptized by fire. The closing of D-Day demonstrated what a highly trained specialized force was capable of accomplishing, but this campaign was far from being over. Prior to dawn on December 4, returning 2nd Regiment patrols reported strong pockets of Panzer grenadiers south of the Remetanea ridge.

The waiting game

1st Company, 3rd Regiment under Capt Gallagher arrived to reinforce the men on top of Difensa; Col Frederick ordered the rest of 1st Battalion, 3rd Regiment to help with the resupply effort. Becket's 1st Battalion, 1st Regiment had not arrived to reinforce 2nd Regiment and their current location was unknown. With strong enemy pockets to the south of Remetanea and the fear of counterattack, Frederick decided to postpone the attack on Hill 907 until dawn on December 5. Throughout the day of December 4, 2nd Regiment sent out several heavy reconnaissance patrols to assess enemy strengths and positions. The fighting continued to go back and forth between the Force and German patrols, as FSSF patrols would move down and encounter German patrols probing upward. It became a test of stamina to see if the Force could hold the mountain.

The conditions on Mt Difensa and the adjoining mountains made patrolling a treacherous business. Dense fog and rain could sometimes clear within moments, exposing soldier's silhouettes against the mountain sky and making them targets for the prying snipers and mortars. The lack of navigable trails was also a hazard, leading to a lot of falls and injuries. German patrols were operating in three- to six-man teams, employing the use of snipers whenever plausible:

> When patrols went out, fighting followed no fixed pattern. The shifting fog enforced a tense alertness on everyone. If fire was opened it was returned on the enemy through the fog. If visibility cleared, all took cover until the patrol leader could size up whether the enemy could be routed, captured, or if it were best to disengage. This situation of a tough enemy on tough terrain makes the dirtiest kind of in-fighting. (Burhans, p.114)

Casualties continued to mount on December 4, not only from the constant patrolling but also from the perpetual mortar fire that seemed to endlessly rain down on Difensa. The German mortar men knew the different ranges on Difensa and were deadly accurate in their fire. The Panzer grenadiers would fire using six-round volleys, then they would adjust their range. The Forcemen came to respect and fear the accuracy with which the Germans mastered the mortar. 1st Battalion commander Maj Ed Thomas would become a casualty that day by jumping into a fox hole during a mortar barrage and landing on one of his men's fixed bayonets, which went through his calf. He would be replaced by Major Walter Gray, 2nd Regiment's executive officer.

The constant patrolling had proved somewhat fruitful, as two German prisoners that were interrogated at about 3:00 pm (1500) indicated that an enemy counterattack was imminent. For a few K-rations, the prisoners divulged that three companies of 3rd Battalion, 104th Panzer Grenadiers would attack Difensa at about 3:00 am (0300) on December 5. This was validated by an artillery observer, who reported about 400 German soldiers massing southwest of Hill 907. 2nd Regiment, 2nd Battalion commander Lt Col Moore affirmed "on the basis of this, artillery covering fire was called to our front to break up a possible assembly of force on the part of the enemy, and the regiment again maintained the alert throughout the night" (cited by Horn and Wyczynski, p.182). The prisoners also indicated that they were having resupply issues as the routes were flooded and the heavy Allied artillery and mortar fire had severely disrupted their mule strength in the forward areas. This information, coupled with the fact that Becket's 1st Battalion, 1st Regiment had yet to arrive on the summit, made Frederick decide to hold off the attack. As the day of December 4 was coming to a close, Frederick reported the following to FSSF Headquarters:

This photograph depicts what were originally labeled as German grenadiers of an unknown unit in Italy, dated December 10, 1943. It is very likely that these may be some of the same soldiers opposing the Fifth Army on the Winter Line. Strangely enough they wear what appear to be airborne smocks with infantry helmets, leading to the possibility that they may be part of the Hermann Göring Division or grenadiers who acquired the smocks. (Bundesarchiv, Bild 183-J16198, photo: Dr. Fochler-Hauke)

> Becket's Bn not arrived except adv party. Wire to WILLIAMSON and to you broken … Present plan is to attack 907 at daylight 5 Dec, provided casualties are low tonight and weather visibility permits. Subjected to hvy mortar & arty fire on top of 960 today, visibility too low to obs origin. Info from PW at 1600 today – Germans assembled 3 additional Companies vicinity 907 today. Increased S/A fire towards LA DIFENSA and our patrols towards 907 bear this out. Expect atk by Germans on LA DIFENSA tonite or early morning. Have held 2 companies of 3rd Regt to reinforce 2nd Regt tonite. (Cited by Joyce, p.161)

The men of the First Special Service Force dug in and braced themselves for another night on Mt Difensa. The rain had ceased, but the downpour of German artillery, Nebelwerfers (also known as Screaming Meemies), and mortar fire would remain constant. The heavy bombardment that Forcemen were suffering under and the heavy patrolling added to the mounting casualties on Difensa. The one glimmer of light for many men on Difensa that evening was that the whiskey ordered by Col Frederick had arrived.

Each man was given a couple of ounces to keep him warm. The men passed the night waiting for the anticipated counterattack that never materialized.

The attack on Mt Remetanea (Hill 907) and the Difensa–Camino Saddle

As the sun rose on December 5, so did Frederick's hopes that he could accomplish his mission of securing Hill 907. Becket's 1st Battalion of 1st Regiment finally arrived and took up 2nd Regiment's defensive positions, allowing 2nd Regiment to be relieved for a short respite and to prepare for an afternoon attack on Remetanea. The men of 2nd Regiment moved on to the southern slopes to dry out in the warm December sun, read the mail that had just arrived and receive a well-deserved rest. As soon as they could be relieved from 36th Division's reserve, Frederick requested the remainder of 1st Regiment, consisting of the 2nd Battalion under Lt Col Jack Akehurst and Col Marshal's headquarters, to make their way to the summit. Frederick also ordered three patrols out to assess the situation. One patrol moved down the saddle southward to try to link up with the British 56th Division, who had yet to take the monastery on Mt Camino. The monastery was heavily defended by two companies of Germans from the 104th Panzer Grenadiers. Most of the German resistance that had plagued the men of the FSSF for the past few days came from the direction of the saddle. Neutralizing the saddle was essential for the success of both the British on Camino and the Force on Difensa. No contact could be made with the British by this patrol, but it was assessed that the 169th Brigade was close to taking all of Camino. The second patrol worked along the ridge toward the eastern slope of Hill 907, where no enemy activity was reported. The final patrol was to make contact with the 142nd Infantry Regiment near the Maggiore heights. The Force patrol trekked all the way to the top of Hill 630 where no contact was made with the 142nd or the enemy. With the fresh intelligence from the patrols now indicating that the German resistance had in fact been weakened, and with the reserves from the 1st Regiment recently arrived, Frederick was prepared to push the attack on to Hill 907.

At 1:00 pm (1300) Maj Gray, with his three companies of 1st Battalion, 2nd Regiment and one company from 3rd Regiment, began to make his push on the northern ridge toward Hill 907. The bulk of the battalion hugged the northern slope, while patrols worked the southern slopes in the direction of the main resistance between Hill 907 and Camino. These patrols came under heavy mortar and machine-gun fire that would soon be directed

A military map detailing Operation *Raincoat* over the 8-day engagement. Absent from this map are 1st and 3rd regiments of the First Special Service Force who both played critical roles in the support of 2nd Regiment in holding Difensa and taking Remetanea. (National Archives)

at the entire battalion, stopping the progress of the whole attack. 1st Battalion, moving over open ground in broad daylight, was forced to dig in halfway to Remetanea on the eastern side of the knoll. Maj Gray sent out patrols in an attempt to locate the enemy pockets while the bulk of his troops had to wait it out until dark. Once again, the saddle area between Camino and Remetanea proved to be a tough nut to crack and the center of German resistance.

At roughly 4:30 pm (1630) Lt Col Moore's 2nd Battalion, 2nd Regiment, with a company from 1st Regiment, moved out southward into the saddle between Difensa and Camino, targeting two knobs, also known as "warts," where the Germans would put up a savage defense. 5th Company under Capt Hubbard spearheaded the assault on the knobs, where the Germans were firmly entrenched; the Forcemen fanned out with bayonets fixed and proceeded cautiously. Under the cover of smoke, the lead company moved towards its objective in twos and threes down the slope until the troops were spotted. Upon reaching the first knob, the Germans opened up with an MG42. The distinctive sound broke the silence and the Forcemen had little choice but to push on through it and take their objectives. The soldiers were now being hit with everything from light and heavy machine guns to mortars, snipers and even the dreaded 88s. The men of 5th Company had no choice but to press the attack, since with the lack of any cover going to the ground would have been suicide, as the mortars would have finished the men off.

With no cover, the men of the Force continued to push the attack on to the makeshift bunkers the Germans had fortified out of holes blasted into the granite. With the 88 and mortar rounds landing all over the place, the Forcemen were able to reach the machine-gun positions and drop grenades into the makeshift holes of the pillboxes.

1st Platoon of 5th Company under Lt Boyce was leading the assault. Using bayonets and grenades, the men followed Lt Boyce as they overwhelmed the first knob by flanking it on three sides. The German defenders, roughly a platoon, at the other now turned their full attention to Boyce and his men. Boyce regrouped his men and led the attack on the second knob. The lieutenant was hit leading the assault, but continued. Boyce then jumped into a German machine-gun nest, using his knife to kill as many of the enemy as possible until he himself was hit by rounds from a machine pistol. Boyce continued to command his men even after suffering several wounds. He died as soon as the knob had been seized.

Moore's 2nd Battalion, 2nd Regiment, unable to make contact with the British and still under German fire from the northern slope of Camino, dug in for the night on the newly acquired knobs. 1st Battalion, 2nd Regiment received very little fire that evening as they dug in waiting for their opportunity to seize Remetanea. Both battalions braced themselves for a potential counterattack. 1st Regiment's Headquarters Company and 2nd Battalion arrived that evening to reinforce Difensa. As the night wore on, the Forcemen were able to watch the British X Corps artillery pour explosives on to the stubborn defenders holed up in the monastery on Hill 963.

MORNING, DECEMBER 5

1st Bn, 1st Regt arrives to reinforce 2nd Regt

The final push

At 10:00 am (1000), Gray's 1st Battalion made its advance on to Mt Remetanea (Hill 907). With harassing machine-gun and mortar fire coming from Camino and the base of Maggiore, the 1st Battalion faced little opposition from the summit. The fight for Remetanea was not nearly as difficult as Difensa due to the full-scale German retreat. Approaching what was essentially a German rearguard, the Forcemen swiftly overwhelmed their bivouac area, taking many by surprise. Men ran out of their tents shooting, just to be quickly killed or captured by the awaiting Forcemen; one Force captain was described as taking 19 prisoners himself. Hill 907 was in Allied hands by noon. Frederick reported, "Have passed crest 907. Will Continue to atk to W, conditions permitting. Radios out of order. Supply priority water, mortar & LMG ammo, rations 2000rds JAR, rifle ammo, blankets & litters" (cited by Joyce, p.162). It was now clear that the intelligence reports from the night before were correct; the Germans had begun to fall back. After consolidating the summit of Hill 907, Gray sent out two companies down the valley towards Rocca d'Evandro. Col Frederick summarized the situation in a communiqué to Gen Walker at 36th Divisional Headquarters:

We have troops down to our left boundary at the saddle and have consolidated for defense of the area south of la Difensa. Our attack to the west against Hill 907 has progressed beyond the crest of 907. We are receiving much machine gun and mortar fire from several directions, principally from the draw running southwest from la Difensa, from the foothills of Maggiore and from the north slopes of Camino. We are endeavoring to place artillery support fire on the troublesome areas but it is difficult due to very low visibility and the British restrictions on our artillery fire. I shall push the attack to the west on past Hill 907 as far as conditions of men will permit. Men are getting in bad shape from fatigue, exposure and cold. Much sickness from a bad batch of K-ration. In accordance last word I have stopped burying dead and am collecting them for Grave Registration Service. German snipers are giving us hell and it is extremely difficult to catch them. They are hidden all throughout the area and shoot bursts at any target. Please press relief of troops from this position as every additional day here will mean two more days of necessary recuperation before next mission. They are willing and eager, but are becoming exhausted. A few officers are talking too much about bad condition of men and I am combating such attitude. Communications are heart-breaking. Mortar fire knock out lines faster than we can repair them. Every time we transmit by radio enemy drops mortar on location. German reinforcements approach up draw southwest of Camino, but I am unable to tell whether they are reinforcing or attempting to organize a counter attack. In my opinion, unless British take Camino before dark today it should be promptly attacked by us from the north. The locations we hold are going to be uncomfortable as long as the enemy holds north slopes of Camino. If supplies have been

Commander of the German XIV Panzer Corps, Generalleutnant Fridolin von Senger und Etterlin, photographed in Italy in the fall of 1943. Von Senger und Etterlin was given command of the XIV Panzer Corps in early October of 1943. The corps consisted of the 15th Panzer Grenadier Division, the 1st Fallschirmjäger Division, the Hermann Göring Division and elements of the 29th Panzer Grenadier Division. Von Senger und Etterlin was directly responsible for defending the Gustav Line, thus placing the Camino mass of Mt Camino and Mt Difensa under the auspices of his command. (Bundesarchiv, Bild 101I-305-0651-26, photo: Dr. Fochler-Hauke)

dropped to us, they have landed too far West, beyond Hill 907 and behind German lines. Do not worry about me or dry clothes for me. I am OK. (Cited by Joyce, p.163)

Throughout the rest of the day, both battalions continued to send out reconnaissance patrols. Occasional sniper and mortar fire plagued the men of the FSSF, but in comparison to the previous nights it was spent in relative ease. On Mt Camino the Germans continued to feel the wrath of the British artillery, as the British 56th Division had been ordered to take the summit at all costs. A II Corps report indicated the position at the close of December 6:

> Enemy situation was generally quiet and static along the front except on our left flank where the enemy is being hard pressed by both the British and us. He has now been driven off most of the heights of the MAGGIORE–DIFENSA hills. In the X Corps sector the British are pushing hard towards Rocca. The enemy finds himself with his back towards the river and its broad mud flats caused by yesterday's flood. His bridges are believed useless to him and his only route of egress from the pocket in which he finds himself is N, directly under our ground observation on MAGGIORE. A counterattack reported as forming in Rocca area at the close of the period [6 December] is born of desperation and is a determined effort to hold at all costs to effect a relief or to withdraw entirely. There may be some truth in the PW's statement n… to the effect that elements of Herman Göring Division may be rushed into the line in order to bolster rapidly weakening defenses. (Cited by Joyce, p.163)

The mop-up

On the morning of December 7, British patrols finally linked up with the 2nd Battalion in the saddle area just south of Difensa, bringing the news that the monastery on Camino had been taken and that X Corps was advancing on Rocca d'Evandro. These encounters were not without incident. One 2nd Regiment patrol was probing the British lines in an attempt to make contact when a firefight erupted in the thick fog as a British patrol opened up on the Forcemen. No casualties were reported and the horrible mistake was quickly rectified. Another patrol of British soldiers liaised with Williamson's 2nd Regiment's headquarters on the summit of Difensa. The rumor was that the British were shocked by the number of majors and colonels that the FSSF had in the forward combat zone. Williamson retorted that the FSSF held to the principle that leaders should lead and that's what Force officers did (Burhans, p.120).

Reports from the 1st Battalion, 2nd Regiment observation posts on Hill 907 indicated that the Germans were in complete withdrawal. Maj Gray ordered his men down the 907 spur to link up with the British on the left flank and the 142nd Infantry on the right towards Maggiore. A dense fog moved in over the valley, making visibility extremely limited. Lt Underhill's platoon stumbled into a large pocket of German resistance about a mile northeast of Rocca. Numbered at roughly 50, the Germans were well armed and equipped. After suffering several casualties,

Lt M. H. (Herb) Goodwin of the 6th Company, 1st Regiment in his Canadian officer uniform with both First Special Service Force and Canadian insignia, taken in December of 1942. Canadian officers in the Force were allowed to keep their Canadian dress uniforms and adorn them with mixed insignia for unofficial use. Once acquired, the US Class A officer uniform was obligatory when on duty, and the only Canadian insignia allowed was a "Canada" collar device. The Canadian officer uniforms could be worn while off duty and on leave. Enlisted men of both nations wore the US Enlisted Class A uniform for dress purposes. (Eric Morgensen /www. firstspecialserviceforce.net)

1630 hrs,
DECEMBER 5

2nd Bn, 2nd Regt
pushes out into
the saddle between
Difensa and
Camino

Underhill ordered his men to withdraw. These Germans, possibly fresh troops from the rear, were there to put up a rearguard action.

The afternoon of December 7 saw FSSF patrols finally gain control of the spur, tying in the positions between Hill 907 and Hill 963. Enemy snipers, now cut off completely from their comrades, continued to play their sinister games within the valley. Col Marshall of 1st Regiment responded by sending out three companies to clear out the last pockets of resistance between Difensa, Remetanea and Camino. Several snipers were killed or captured during the afternoon, neutralizing their threat. For the first night since the climb, the men of the FSSF were able to rest in relative ease within their positions on Difensa, Remetanea, and the forward saddle area, yet they were always wary of possible counterattack. The 2nd Canadian Parachute Regiment War Diary for December 7 summarized the day as follows:

> Bright and fairly warm. Another list of wounded received. It is known that 115 have been evacuated through one advance evacuation hospital to Naples, others being brought in as fast as they can get them down. It takes 10 men to bring down one stretcher case and takes them the best part of the day, the mountain is so precipitous, all able bodied men are needed for combat. The Air Corps has made one or two unsuccessful attempts to drop supplies of food, water and ammunition to advance groups who are right out and the supply lines can't get to them. (Cited by Wood, p.203)

That night 36th Division headquarters began to make preparations for the withdrawal of the First Special Service Force.

On December 8, the last objective was to clear out the roughly 50-man German rearguard that was encountered by Lt Underhill's platoon the previous day. With artillery coordination and clear visibility, Maj Gray sent his battalion down the ridge towards the last pocket of German resistance. With a rolling barrage preceding the men of the FSSF, they were able to quickly neutralize the enemy with few casualties. Twenty-five Germans were killed and seven taken prisoner, and the rest retreated. This last group of German resistance was confirmed as fresh troops from the Hermann Göring Division. The First Special Service Force had completed its mission, enemy activity had completely ceased, and after six days of continuous fighting the only thing left to do was to be relieved.

Withdrawal and reflection

At about 8:00 pm (2000) two battalions of the 142nd Infantry began to arrive at the top of Difensa to relieve the men of the FSSF. Throughout the night the Forcemen wearily made their way down the mountain. An onlooker commented, "they all looked alike … Their faces were gray, expressionless, and their clothes caked with mud and blood" (cited by Horn and Wyczynski, p.184). Prior to the attack, many of the men of the 36th Division had wondered who and what the First Special Service Force was and why they thought they could take Difensa when so many others had failed. For three months, the men of the Fifth Army had tried to take Difensa without success; as the Forcemen passed through the lines of 36th Division on the way down

1200 hrs,
DECEMBER 6

Mt Remetanea (Hill
907) is in FSSF
hands

the mountain, a silence hung over the onlookers. Many were astonished and looked on in disbelief, but the men of the First Special Service Force knew this was what they were trained for, to accomplish the impossible; they were just exhausted and fatigued. Many from 2nd Regiment were unable to walk back down the mountain, since 2nd Regiment had suffered the heaviest casualties in the Difensa campaign, many of the wounded being hit several times. Some of the Forcemen that could walk were amazed at their own accomplishments; many looking for the first time at the mountain in daylight were shocked that they were able to negotiate the narrow paths, the sheer cliffs and the ropes at night and in such secrecy. For many, the magnitude of the situation was just becoming clear. On the morning of December 9 the weary men of the Force boarded trucks for transit back to the barracks at Santa Maria. The December 9 entry of the War Diary recalls: "The 2nd Regiment began to arrive about 0200 hours, the showers were in operation as were the kitchens. The men though extremely tired perked up considerably after getting cleaned up and a hot breakfast. The 3rd Regiment and Service Battalion arrived during the morning and by noon practically everyone who was not casualty had arrived" (cited by Wood, p.203).

Lt Gen Mark Clark was given command of the Fifth Army for the invasion of Italy and the drive to Rome. Clark was responsible for the Allied push through the Winter Line, the landings at Anzio and the drive towards and the taking of Rome. The First Special Service Force served under Clark until being transferred to the First Airborne Task Force in August of 1944. Clark has been criticized by many historians for not using the FSSF in an appropriate manner. Instead of using the Force as the highly skilled and trained commando force that it was, Clark insisted on deploying it as shock or assault infantry. While effective, this tactic decimated the ranks of the highly trained force time and time again. (Library of Congress)

Col Frederick received two communications from headquarters on December 10. The first was from Lt Gen Mark Clark, commander of the Fifth Army:

To: The Commanding Officer:

1. I desire to commend the officers and men of the First Special Service Force for the part they played in recent operations.

2. The Special Service Force was given the task of capturing la Difensa, an extremely difficult piece of high ground in the Mt Maggiore hill mass, the possession of which was vital to our further advance in that sector. The mission was carried out at night in spite of adverse weather conditions and heavy enemy rifle, machine-gun, mortar, and artillery fires on precipitous slopes over which it was necessary to attack. Furthermore, the position was maintained despite counterattacks and difficulties of communication and supply. The fact that you have acquitted yourself well in your first action under enemy fire is a tribute to fine leadership and a splendid reward for time spent in arduous training.

Mark W. Clark

Lt General, U.S.A.

Commanding Fifth Army. (Cited by Burhans, p.124)

The other letter was from Maj Gen Geoffrey Keyes, II Corps commander:

I am fully cognizant of the stubbornness of the enemy and the difficulties of weather and terrain encountered in the seizure of Mt. Difensa and Hill 907, and of the bravery, fortitude, and resourcefulness with which your command overcame them. It is with genuine anticipation that I look forward to your next assignment under my command.

Sincerely,

Geoffrey Keyes

Major General, U.S.A.

Commanding II Corps. (Cited by Burhans, p.125)

During the six-day campaign, the First Special Service Force suffered 73 dead, 9 missing, 313 wounded and 116 exhaustion cases, roughly equaling 25 percent of the Force's combat strength. The Canadian War Diary of December 10 concluded, "at this rate the Canadian element which is not being reinforced will not survive many like missions" (cited by Burhans, p.124).

The campaign continues

The First Special Service Force was pulled out of the line for 11 days for a much-needed rest, yet the operation was far from over. Fifth Army began Phase II of its attack on the Winter Line starting on December 9, this time focusing on the mountains north of the Mignano Gap. Mt Sammucro, Mt Lungo, and the town of San Pietro were the primary German strongholds. II Corps again led the assault, as the British X Corps held the Camino Mass and VI Corps feinted to the North. The 1st Italian Motorized Group attacked Mt Lungo, while the 3rd Ranger Battalion and the 1st Battalion of the 143rd Infantry attacked the summit of Mt Sammucro. Two battalions of the 143rd then pushed for the high ground above San Pietro. The German defenders fought back viciously in this sector, counterattacking at every opportunity. Mt Lungo and San Pietro eventually fell after weeks of fighting; the summit of Mt Sammucro was also taken but the Germans still held the hills below, most importantly Hill 720. The Germans also held Mt Vischiataro and Mt Majo north of the Sammucro mass.

Lt Cuddy leads a platoon of men from 5th Company, 3rd Regiment through the mountains near Mt Majo sometime between January 1 and 17, 1944. Majo was the next large objective for the Force after Difensa. Lt Cuddy would die of wounds suffered at Anzio a few weeks later. (National Archives)

On December 21, the First Special Service Force was again deployed from its barracks at Santa Maria with the task of taking Mt Majo and Mt Vischiataro. Before this could be accomplished, Hill 720 had to be cleared, and 1st Regiment was given this task. At 2:00 am (0200) on Christmas Day 1943, 1st Regiment attacked from the heights of Sammucro downhill towards the Germans. The fighting was intense and personal and turned into a hand-to-hand struggle, but by 7:00 am (0700) the Force held Hill 720. On January 3, 1944 the 2nd Regiment with the remaining 1st Regiment started a sweep through the Radicosa hills. On the 4th the 3rd Regiment set out in a two-pronged attack to take Mt Majo and Mt Vischiataro, becoming fully committed to the attack on the 6th. On the 7th the 1st Regiment attacked Monte Majo; many of the Forcemen began to run out of ammunition and were forced to use captured weapons to push the Germans off the mountain. The Germans counterattacked more than 40 times, to no avail. By January 17, Radicosa, Mt Majo, and Mt Vischiataro were secure and the Force was being withdrawn.

The Force not only fought the Germans, but had to fight the below freezing temperatures, snow, fatigue, and hunger. Of the original 1,800 in the combat echelon, 1,400 were either dead, wounded, or recovering from weather-related injuries. The Service Battalion was also roughly at half strength, with Frederick pulling men out to fight in the combat ranks. The First Special Service Force was now well under half strength and in need of replacements. It was questionable if the Force would continue.

The First Special Service Force would indeed continue, however, as less well-trained replacements filled its depleted ranks. On February 2, 1944, the First Special Service Force landed on the Anzio beachhead. The Anzio landings were designed to bypass the Winter Line for a quick drive on to Rome. Anzio became an entrenched 30-mile defensive perimeter. It was at Anzio that the remnants of Darby's Rangers, the 1st, 3rd, and 4th Ranger Battalions, were assigned to the Force as replacements. On the right flank of the Mussolini Canal, the 1st Regiment dug in, in holding three miles. The 3rd Regiment held five miles next to the 1st Regiment's positions. The 2nd Regiment was held as a reserve force behind the lines. The Force now actively held eight miles of the front itself, but it did not sit idle in a defensive situation. Col Fredrick, now a brigadier general, ordered reconnaissance patrols, harassment raids, night raids, and other offensive tactics that demoralized the enemy and energized the men of the Force. 2nd Regiment

Three members of 4th Company, 2nd Regiment photographed with an unknown Commonwealth soldier in Casablanca. The previously mentioned Harold "Ted" Johnson is on the left, Mayberry is seated and Chester May from McMinnville, Oregon is standing on the right. Johnson was wounded on the summit of Mt Difensa on the morning of the December 4 while trying to make a quick breakfast. During an artillery barrage a piece of shrapnel went through his shoulder and collapsed one of his lungs. Still conscious, Johnson made his way back down the mountain refusing a stretcher, later stating to his family that he "still had two good legs and some boys needed the stretcher more than he did." Johnson was found by Lt Bill Story of 4th Co., 2nd Reg that night stumbling around at the base of Difensa, having lost a lot of blood after the day-long walk down the mountain. Johnson was taken to North Africa for medical treatment, where he cheated his way through his physical so that he could rejoin the FSSF in Italy. (The Johnson Family)

A Force patrol of the Headquarters Detachment enters the town of Cervaro on January 15, 1944 after a difficult few weeks in the Radicosa area. Sgt Charles Russell with the Thompson SMG covers Pvt Barney Wright and an unidentified Forceman as they search for snipers. Moments after this photograph was taken, the unidentified Forceman and Pvt Wright were killed by the sought-after snipers. (National Archives)

was given the primary task of conducting these intense night raids into enemy territory; the purpose was to give the Germans the impression that there was an entire division on the canal.

On May 23, 1944, the First Special Service Force spearheaded the Anzio breakout and the drive on to Rome. The men went over the top at the Mussolini Canal, fighting across open country against German armor, artillery, and well-disciplined infantry. Town by town the Force led the way during the Anzio breakout, where they encountered very intense resistance. Rome was liberated on June 4, 1944; members of the FSSF were some of the first to enter the city.

The Force left Italy in the summer of 1944 to join the First Airborne Task Force for the invasion of southern France, where it enjoyed a series of victories until it was disbanded in December. The Italian campaign would have been very different without the efforts of the First Special Service Force.

ANALYSIS

By most accounts, the raid on Mt Difensa by the First Special Service Force was an overwhelming success. It enabled the Fifth Army to gain control of the southern heights over the Liri Valley, considered by many to be the gateway to Rome. Difensa was the key to the entire Camino mass area; without it, none of the other objectives could have been taken or held. The FSSF did in hours what other regiments could not do in months. This is not to say that mistakes were not made, or causalities were not high, or that the failure of the Germans to counterattack in force did not play a factor in the outcome of the engagement. What Mt Difensa did prove was that a highly-trained group of very motivated soldiers could accomplish what many would consider impossible.

0200 hrs, DECEMBER 9

2nd Regt arrives back at its barracks in Santa Maria

Forcemen receive doughnuts and coffee from the Red Cross at the Santa Maria barracks on January 19, 1944, during a much-needed rest after their campaigns in the Winter Line. The Force's next stop would be the Anzio beachhead. (National Archives)

Lessons learned

Mt Difensa was the First Special Service Force's baptism by fire, and many lessons were learned that would be studied and utilized by not only the forces in Italy but by future generations of Special Forces from both the United States and Canada. In an 18-page restricted First Special Service Force memorandum entitled *Lessons from the Italian Campaign* dated April 14, 1944, several key tactical lessons were addressed regarding the fighting on Difensa and the Winter Line:

2. Terrain

Of particular interest to us are the limitations and peculiarities of high, rugged, mountainous country. In such country terrain alone affects almost every phase of operations, e.g. routes of approach, flank security, tactics, supply, care and evacuation of wounded and communications ... To this must be added the limitations imposed by severe weather conditions where rain, mud, and cold added to the difficulties of movement, supply, and health ... The most important single lesson learned from the terrain covered was that without exception high ground must be taken and held ... We soon found that whenever the enemy held the ground above, whenever he had as much as one observer who was located on a dominant feature, we suffered from his mortar and artillery fire ... We learned beyond any shadow of doubt that fighting in this mountainous terrain required the highest degree of physical fitness for all ranks. Not only the combat soldier, but supply train personnel, stretcher bearers, staff officers, and runners, all required great physical stamina.

3. Attack

c. Reconnaissance: Before any attack can be made and any night patrol sent out, reconnaissance is essential to its complete success ... e. Field and Small-Group Tactics: ... All our engagements have confirmed the most important single principle of infantry combat – the effective use of fire and movement ... f. The following of artillery fires and concentrations: This Force learned early in its combat experience of the advantage and necessity of following closely the line of impact of its supporting artillery concentrations and barrages. Terrain and other conditions affect this considerably. Where the attack is up the steep slope of a high mountain mass as at la Difensa, it is almost impossible to employ anything in the nature of a creeping barrage and any barrage laid down has to be either on the ridge or the plateau at the top or on the slopes well forward of the advancing troops ... This has resulted in very heavy barrages being laid on the ridges some considerable time before the assaulting troops were in position to attack. The enemy were little effected by the barrage because of their bunkers and defensive positions and were found to be alert and active again by the time the assault went in ... h. Consolidation: Our experience has been that enemy forces launch an immediate counterattack whenever possible in order to regain ground lost, and precede this attack with mortar and artillery fire. Very often this fire proved to be extremely accurate and of heavy concentration and would fall on the vacated enemy positions and on the ridge lines, both good targets for registered fire. Consequently, the need for immediate and efficient consolidation is obvious.

8. Enemy Tactics and Weapons

An officer of the 1st Regiment who saw action on Mount la Difensa noted from his observation of enemy outposts and snipers that they sited their outposts, usually manned by two men with a MG or MP, with an additional sniper in a well concealed position some 50–100 yards to the left of the outpost. The reason for this appeared to be that when the outpost fired their automatic weapons (often simply into the air to attract our fire) our riflemen would show themselves always to the right of their own cover, because their natural body-positions for firing is that of fire from the right shoulder. This exposed our rifleman to the lone enemy sniper located on the left of the enemy outpost.

10. Miscellaneous

b. Medical Evacuation: In our engagements in rugged mountainous country we rapidly learned the necessity of departing from the normal in the situating of aid posts. The extreme difficulty in evacuating wounded over precipitous trails, in darkness and under fire, with the delay involved, rendered it necessary to put aid stations almost as far to the front as the forward troops, if adequate medical aid was to be rendered in sufficient time. This practice was adopted very early in our engagements. The difficulties of terrain also required many more stretcher-bearers than are normally employed, and it often became necessary to use reserve combat troops to the point of exhaustion in order to accomplish efficient evacuation of the wounded. c. Physical Fitness: The need for physical fitness of the highest order by all personnel has been stressed in the discussion of mountain warfare. It cannot be over emphasized. Demands much above accepted peak performance are made suddenly and without warning. Will and determination alone are not enough. The necessary physical strength must be there. And it was soon found that it must be there in every man in the command not alone in the combat soldier. (Ross, pp.181–85)

These lessons learned would prove vital in the continued success of First Special Service Force operations throughout the rest of the war, as well as setting a standard for future mountain operations for both the Special Forces of the United States and Canada.

Morale

As their first combat engagement, the raid on Mt Difensa secured the First Special Service Force's place in history. This event had a tremendous impact on the morale of the men, demonstrating that their intense specialized style of training did in fact make them some of the most elite soldiers in the war. The personal selection process of their recruitment, the use of superior tactics, and the advanced physical and mental conditioning, all of which were a byproduct of almost a year of constant training, were what many considered to be the secret behind the success of the Force. Combat was their job, it was what they were trained to do and they did it professionally and without hesitation. For many Forcemen, Difensa demystified the notion of the

Lt Kostelec of 1st Company, 3rd Regiment, is photographed a month after the raid on Mt Difensa on January 2, 1944. Notice that his lieutenant bars have been embroidered on to his M43 field coat. Kostelec, originally from Calgary, Alberta, was reported missing in action in Anzio on March 4, 1944, and was presumed dead. (Lt Frederick G. Whitecombe/ Canada. Dept. of National Defense/Library and Archives Canada/ Pa-183879)

Germans as the superlative soldiers of the world. According to Sgt Riggs of 2nd Regiment, "The Germans I saw were just like me, but we were better. After Difensa I never met a German I was afraid of" (Springer, p.117).

The men may not have felt very heroic directly following the campaign, as exhaustion and the high casualty rates weighed heavily on their minds. It would not be long, however, before the Forcemen soon realized the amazing achievements they had just accomplished. Correspondent Clark Lee testified, "This feat captured the imagination of the entire Fifth Army and overnight Frederick and his soldiers became almost legendary figures in a battle area where heroism was commonplace ... The Difensa attack is destined to live in military annals because of the endurance, daring and fighting skill it involved" (Adleman and Walton, pp.145–46).

The memorandum *Lessons from the Italian Campaign* of April 14, 1944 detailed the importance of morale, and unlike other outfits that might require hot meals, clean clothes and sheets, being relieved from the front for appropriate periods of time, and the occasional USO show to boost the spirits of their men, the officers of the Force focused on a different recipe for success. While the basic needs of the men were of course addressed for achieving high morale, the idea of victory played the largest role in the spirits of the men of the FSSF:

> The best antidotes found in our combat experience appear to be aggressive action however limited in scope, new combat tasks whenever possible, opportunity to rest at regular intervals, hot food at every available opportunity and sound unit discipline with its resultant pride in appearance of personnel and lines. The most important single factor in morale is victory in battle. It matters little how small the battle is. It is the simple fact that victory over his enemy is what counts with every man. (Cited by Ross, p.185)

Members of 4th Company, 2nd Regiment photographed in southern France in the fall of 1944. Some of these men, such as Ted Johnson, seated second from right in the front row, were original Forcemen from the training in Helena, MT, and others were replacements filling the ranks left vacant after Difensa, Majo and Anzio. 4th Company, 2nd Battalion, 2nd Regiment followed the 1st Battalion up the ropes during the Difensa campaign on December 3rd, suffered heavy casualties while holding on the 4th, and attacked down the saddle between Difensa and Camino on the 5th, again taking heavy casualties. (The Johnson Family)

With regard to the men's morale when faced with casualties, it was noted, "the lesson learned is that the answer to the problem lies in psychological hardening training by all commanders, and efforts of the leader on the spot to transfer any feelings of confusion and alarm into immediate aggressiveness and revenge" (Cited by Ross, p.185). These lessons in morale would be utilized time and time again with the men of the First Special Service Force, as 1st Lt Michaelson of 2nd Regiment described: "We were trained to destroy, and we destroyed everything. We were a bunch of crazy men. Nuts! No fear at all" (Springer, p.167). Mt Difensa made the men of the Force legendary, and time and time again throughout the rest of the war the men of the Force would live up to this reputation, never losing a battle and instilling fear in the enemy everywhere they went.

The sacking of 2nd Regiment's commander

Not everyone walked away from Difensa regarded as a conqueror. 2nd Regiment's commanding officer Col Williamson, the man who led the raiding regiment, would not find his career on the fast track to promotions and decorations as one would think, but in complete ruin as result of the raid. Immediately following the assault, Col Frederick wrote Lt Col Don Williamson up for the Legion of Merit for his regiment's actions during the campaign. This recommendation would soon be repealed, however, based on Williamson's reported actions during the first 24 hours of the Difensa campaign. Five signed affidavits from 2nd Regiment's staff indicated that Williamson had become panicky at the beginning of the fighting. It is reported that he was afraid to go forward when seeking a command post prior to the climb. While based at the bottom of the ropes after 1st Battalion had engaged the enemy on the summit, Williamson started to fire irrationally up at a sniper with his pistol. While on the summit it was stated that Williamson never left his CP in a cave, that the forward positions were never inspected and that he was extremely fearful of a counterattack. Maj Gray stated, "it was necessary for Lt Col Moore and myself to more or less take over and actually make decisions" (Joyce, p.175). The December 31, 1943, *1. Canadian Army Overseas, Officers Confidential Report* made by Frederick indicates:

> As a result of his performance during recent combat operations, personnel under his command have lost confidence in him and do not regard him with respect which a senior officer and combat commander must hold. Without his subordinates' confidence and respect, and because of his evident lack of leadership, I cannot retain him in the capacity of a senior commander. I feel that he is emotionally and temperamentally unfitted for combat duty. (Cited by Joyce, p.176)

Williamson, who admitted to being "jittery," never believed that he acted in any other way than in a professional manner. In his rebuttal to the report he stated, "I acted at all times in accordance with sound military principles, both tactically and administratively" (Joyce, p.177). Many officers and peers within the Force believed Williamson to be a good officer and not guilty of any wrongdoing. 1st Regiment's commander Marshal wrote, "I am firmly convinced that he did a competent job, that he handled his subordinate units well and that there was no doubt as to the ultimate success of the operation" (Joyce, p.179). Williamson was never given a chance to clear his name and his requests for an official inquiry were disregarded. He was soon sent back to Canada. For many, it was a sad day to see their commander and friend leave. Several officers and men wrote in defense of Williamson, but it was too late. The War Diary entry for January 1, 1944 states:

> Colonel Williamson came in from the front in the afternoon, he had been called into the Force Commander's C.P. in the morning, shown statements signed by some of his regimental officers, declaring lack of confidence in him as a result of the La Difensa operation four weeks ago … He was asked how quickly he could be packed and leave as he had been relieved from his command. He had no opportunity to defend himself – a most unfair way to handle the case and especially to treat the man who had helped to create the Force and who has been at the helm through its many turbulent and trying times. (Wood, p.205)

It may never be known as to whether Williamson acted in an unfit manner; Frederick at first certainly did not think so when writing him up for the Legion of Merit. On the other hand, Frederick was also well aware that a lack of confidence in an officer could undermine the entire Force; thus he took the steps he believed were necessary to maintain combat efficiency within the organization by removing Williamson.

A short-lived victory

Most historians concur that Operation *Raincoat* was a success and the role of the First Special Service Force in the Winter Line campaign was the key to that success. Rome, of course, was the main Allied objective in the Italian Campaign. The Gustav Line, more specifically Mt Cassino, was the main obstacle in achieving that objective; without taking Difensa and later Remetanea, Cassino could not have been touched by the Allied forces. Chief Intelligence Officer Burhans later stated, "The Force seizure of first the la Difensa eminence and later la Remetanea had sealed the German doom on the whole mass … On the lower extension of the mass, Maggiore, the German defense lost all hope of holding that poor ground once the overlooking heights had been scaled and captured by the Force. As the fight developed it had become plain that Difensa was the key to the Allied success across the whole mass" (Burhans, p.123). Other historians have agreed that "a major advance was rendered virtually certain by the Force's victory. Difensa was the key to the later success of all the Allied armies in that part of Italy" (Adleman and Walton, p.145) and that "Operation *Raincoat* was definitely a success. In nine days II Corps and X Corps had driven the enemy from practically the entire Camino feature; Fifth Army now controlled the heights on one side of the corridor which gives access to the Liri Valley" (US War Dept, p.28).

The question is often asked why the Germans did not counterattack prior to the First Special Service Force's consolidation of the mountain. The reality of the situation was that after the initial raid on Difensa, 2nd Regiment was

Forcemen on the French–Italian border, fall of 1944. Reminiscent of the early days in Italy, the Force ended its career in the mountains just as it had begun. Following the invasion of southern France, the Force swept across the Riviera neutralizing pockets of strong resistance, eventually arriving in the mountains of the French–Italian border region. The Force was disbanded following this campaign, with the Americans forming the bulk of the 474th Infantry Regiment (Separate) and the Canadians forming the 1st Canadian Special Service Battalion and later being split among various units such as the 1st Canadian Parachute Battalion. Here Red Jones (facing the camera) and Thomas Philips (with his back to the camera), both of 2nd Company, 1st Regiment, are seen as a patrol returns in the background. (Author's Collection/FSSFLHG)

severely weakened, low on supplies, ammunition, and was lacking reinforcements. A strong and organized German counterattack might have had the potential to dislodge the new victors. Several factors played into the German inability to counterattack; first, the Rapido and Garigliano rivers had flooded their banks, taking out the bridges that were essential to the German resupply effort; and second, the Allied artillery had been detrimental to the Panzer grenadiers that had been stationed in defense of the Camino mass area. Considering these two factors, Field Marshal Kesselring decided it was best to fight a delaying action on the southern anchor of the Winter Line as opposed to assigning troops to an area he could not resupply. By fighting a rearguard action in the Difensa–Camino area, Kesselring enabled his crack troops such as the Hermann Göring Division to dig in north of Highway 6 in defense of Cassino.

In the short term the campaign was a success. It achieved the sought objectives and the First Special Service Force distinguished itself as an elite fighting force. The overall Allied strategy to crack the Gustav Line was in fact a failure, however, leading to the Anzio landings that were intended to bypass the impenetrable German defensive line. General Clark, General Keyes and other top commanders were convinced that if Difensa fell the entire Gustav Line would crumble, thus opening the Liri Valley. Many felt it would then be a matter of weeks before the Allies were triumphantly marching through Rome. The reality was of course much different. The Force would continue to slug it out for weeks in the mountains of the Winter Line with the rest of the Fifth Army. Mt Cassino proved to be a formidable defense that would hold up the Allies for months and the Liri Valley did not end up being the super highway into Rome that Clark had hoped. Thus there was the need for the landings at Anzio in February of 1944 to bypass the Winter Line, where the FSSF would find itself again distinguishing itself in combat and doing the job of a much larger unit.

CONCLUSION

The raid itself on Mt Difensa by the First Special Service Force was a military success by all measures. The surprise raid allowed the Force to overwhelm and rout the German defenders in just hours, and created a ripple effect throughout the Camino mass. With the Germans off Mt Difensa, the British were able eventually to take Camino and the 142nd Infantry were able to gain control of Maggiore. Operation *Raincoat* was an Allied victory, opening the Mignano Gap from the south and consequently allowing the Fifth Army to continue the attack north of the Gap and Highway 6. After hearing what happened on Difensa, Winston Churchill stated, "If we had a dozen like him [Frederick], we would have smashed Hitler in 1942. He's the greatest general of all time" (cited by Horn and Wyczynski, p.185). The First Special Service Force was one of the few units in the world that had the capability to pull off such an operation; the sad fact is that it would never be used again in a capacity that matched its skills and training.

Mt Difensa was in many ways the defining event for many in the First Special Service Force. For most Forcemen it was their first combat experience; it proved that their training and commitment had paid off. Difensa is also the perfect example of what can be achieved by using special operations forces. Eisenhower stated in his postwar book *Crusade in Europe*:

> In the mountain passes the Germans constructed defenses almost impregnable to attack. Yankee ingenuity and resourcefulness were tested to the limit. Shortly after the capture of Mt Camino, I was taken to a spot where, in order to outflank one of these mountain strongpoints, a small detachment had put on a remarkable exhibition of mountain climbing. With the aid of ropes, a few of them climbed steep cliffs of great height. I have never understood how, encumbered by their equipment, they were able to do it. In fact, I think that any Alpine climber would have examined the place doubtfully before attempting to scale it. Nevertheless, the detachment reached the top and ferreted out the German Company Headquarters. They entered and seized the captain, who ejaculated, "You can't be here. It is impossible to come up those rocks." (Eisenhower, p.203)

Although he did not mention the unit by name, it is very clear to whom he was referring.

Gen Clark had at his disposal an elite special operations force that would never be properly employed as such. Clark used the First Special Service Force as assault infantry or shock troops time and time again in the Italian Campaign. This tactic bled the Force terribly, and was considered a waste of their training by many. The December 31, 1943 entry of the 2nd Canadian Parachute Regiment War Diary sums it up best:

> [The Force] … finds itself in a definitely secondary theater being used as glorified infantry and all the special training going by the boards, except possibly for mountain climbing. The question that can only be answered in the new year is "will the Force be permitted to peter out here, which it is doing rapidly, or will it be employed in a new theater where some of its specialized training can be used to advantage?" (Cited by Wood, p.204)

The prediction would come true to some extent; the Force was back in action just weeks after Difensa, slugging it through the northern mountains of the Mignano Gap, taking mountain after mountain. The Force was then sent to Anzio, where it held a portion of the beachhead that was normally reserved for an entire division. It was here that the Germans began to truly fear these "black devils," the raiders of the night. The Force spearheaded the Anzio breakout and the drive to Rome, being the first into the eternal city. The Force would again be called on to make amphibious landings by taking out two island forts for the invasion of southern France.

The First Special Service Force never retreated and never lost a battle, and ended up with a combat record that is second to none. The legacy of the Force continues to this day, as both the US Special Forces and the Canadian Special Operations Regiment still carry the battle honors of the Force. The fact that it was never used to its capability is now in the past, as Frederick and his First Special Service Force have etched their place in history as the founding fathers of American and Canadian Special Forces.

BIBLIOGRAPHY AND FURTHER READING

Books

Adleman, Robert H., and Walton, George, *The Devil's Brigade*, Chilton Books (Philadelphia and New York, 1966)

Burhans, Robert D., *The First Special Service Force: A War History of the North Americans 1942–1944*, The Battery Press (Nashville, 1947)

Cottingham, Peter Layton, *Once Upon A Wartime: A Canadian Who Survived the Devil's Brigade*, Prairie Mountain Publishers Inc Brandon (Manitoba, 1996)

Eisenhower, Dwight D., *Crusade in Europe*, Doubleday and Company, Inc (Garden City, NY, 1948)

Horn, Colonel Bernd and Wyczynski, Michel, *Of Courage and Determination: The First Special Service Force, "The Devil's Brigade," 1942–44*, Dundurn Press (Toronto, 2013)

Joyce, Kenneth, *Snow Plough and the Jupiter Deception: The First Special Service Force and the 1st Canadian Special Service Battalion, 1943–1945*, Vanwell Publishing Ltd (St Catherines, Ontario, 2006)

Joyce, Ken, *Crimson Spearhead, First Special Service Force: History, Uniforms, Insignia*, Service Publications (Ottawa, 2010)

Nadler, John, *A Perfect Hell: The True Story of the Black Devils, the Forefathers of the Special Forces*, Presidio Press (New York, 2006)

Ross, Robert Todd, *The Supercommandos: First Special Service Force, 1942–1944 An Illustrated History*, Schiffer Publishing (Atglen, Philadelphia, 2000)

Springer, Joseph A., *The Black Devil Brigade: The True Story of the First Special Service Force: An Oral History*, Pacifica Military History (Pacifica, California, 2001)

Werner, Bret, *First Special Service Force 1942–44*, Osprey Publishing (Oxford, 2006)

Wood, James A., *We Move Only Forward: Canada, the United States and the First Special Service Force 1942–1944*, Vanwell Publishing Ltd (St Catherines, Ontario, 2006)

US War Department, *The Fifth Army at the Winter Line, 15 Nov 1943 – 15 Jan 1944*, American Forces in Action Series (Washington, DC: Government Printer, 1945)

Websites

http://www.firstspecialserviceforce.net/ First Special Service Force Association

INDEX